IN ORDER TO GET INFORMATION OUT, YOU NEED TO BE ABLE TO GET DATA IN...

D1217178

§sas. | SAS Publishing

Reading External Data Files Using SAS®:
EXAMPLES HANDBOOK

Michele M. Burlew

The Power to Know.

The correct bibliographic citation for this manual is as follows: Burlew, Michele M. 2002. *Reading External Data Files Using SAS®: Examples Handbook*. Cary, NC: SAS Institute Inc.

Reading External Data Files Using SAS®: Examples Handbook

TABLE OF CONTENTS

Chapter 4- Operating System Specific Features When Reading External Files

ACKNOWLEDGMENTS

Thanks to Books by Users Press for the opportunity to write this book. I love working with data and I enjoyed creating examples of the many ways of reading external data files with SAS.

Thanks to Julie Platt, Acquisitions Editor, for her continued great advice on how to write for the SAS audience and for her management of the project. Thanks to Brad Kellam who led the copyediting, to Candy Farrell who produced the book, to Beth Heinig for design of the book, and to Patricia Spain and Cindy Puryear for marketing.

Finally, I want to acknowledge the contributions of time, effort, and commitment made by the technical reviewers. I greatly appreciate their detailed reviews, suggestions, and availability for questions. Thanks to the technical reviewers: Amber Elam, Carol Linden, Kevin Hobbs, Charley Mullin, Ginny Piechota, Randy Poindexter, Andy Ravenna, Jason Secosky, Jean Ussery, and Cynthia Zender.

CHAPTER 1
AN INTRODUCTION TO READING RAW DATA WITH SAS

Overview

The goal when reading an external data file is to create a SAS data set or data view that SAS can process to produce meaningful reports and analyses. This book presents examples of reading external data files and instream data that you can adapt to read your own data. This chapter presents the concepts of reading these data sources with SAS.

Collectively, unprocessed data stored in an external data file or included as part of the job stream are termed raw data. DATA steps read raw data and create SAS data sets and views from the raw data. With the features of the INFILE and INPUT SAS language statements, you describe to SAS the structure of your raw data. You can also specify attributes of an external data file in the FILENAME statement.

As considered in this book, external files contain unprocessed data not stored in a SAS data set. These files can transfer information between software applications and the structures of these files can vary. External files are managed by your operating system, not by SAS. Depending on your operating system, you may refer to your external files as flat files, text files, sequential files, DAT files, or ASCII files.

There is an endless variety of ways in which to store raw data. For example, an external file from a clinical study could contain one data line for one patient for one set of lab tests. Another way of representing the same information is to write a series of data lines for one patient: the first data line contains the patient identifiers and is followed by several data lines, each data line containing the patient's results from a lab test. A third way to create this clinical study file is to place information for multiple patients in each data line. A patient identifier is followed by the lab test results. The information for the next patient continues on the same data line.

Most examples in this book show how to read raw data stored in external files. Another way to read raw data is to include the data as part of the job stream. A few examples of reading instream data are presented in this chapter.

Methods of Reading Raw Data

SAS has several ways of reading raw data. These include

❏ SAS language statements in the DATA step

❏ SAS functions

❏ the Import Wizard and the External File Interface (EFI)

❏ the SAS procedure IMPORT.

The INFILE statement describes the attributes of the external file containing the raw data that you want the DATA step to read. The INFILE statement can either directly name the external file or it can indirectly point to the external file with a fileref defined with the FILENAME statement or window. Typical attributes that you might specify in the INFILE statement are the delimiter between fields and the record length.

With the INPUT statement, you describe to SAS the structure of your data. An INPUT statement that uses simple list input may be able to read your external file by scanning the data lines for data values if your data values are separated by at least one delimiter such as a space. On the other hand, your external file may not have delimiters between data values and the data values may have a specific structure. To read that external file, you may need to use a different INPUT style, such as column input or formatted input.

SAS functions can also read and write external files. These functions either can be coded in a DATA step or can be used outside of the DATA step in the SAS macro language.

If you are running SAS in an interactive windowing environment such as Windows, UNIX, or OpenVMS, you can use the Import Wizard and the EFI to read and write external files. These features use a point-and-click interface that prompt you for information about your external files.

Also available under the SAS windowing environments listed above is the SAS procedure IMPORT. This PROC reads external files as well as tables in database management systems. PROC IMPORT can run in SAS interactive mode as well as in batch mode.

Understanding Data Sources

The way you write your DATA step depends on where your data are stored. Your raw data may be in one of two locations:

❒ part of the job stream

❒ stored in an external file.

Most examples in this book show how to read data stored in external files.

Reading Data That is Part of the Job Stream

Raw data that is part of the job stream follows the DATA step code that reads it. You would typically select this style of programming only if you were processing small amounts of data. Either a DATALINES or DATALINES4 statement precedes the raw data.

If you maintain older SAS programs, you may see the CARDS or CARDS4 statement instead of DATALINES or DATALINES4.

In the example that follows, a DATA step reads six variables from five data lines. The data lines are part of the job stream.

Example 1.1 Reading Instream Data Lines

```
data runners;
   input name $ age runtime1 runtime2 runtime3 runtime4;
datalines;
Scott 15 23.3 21.5 22.0 21.9
Mark 13 25.2 24.1 23.5 22.0
Jon 13 25.1 25.7 24.3 25.0
Michael 14 24.6 24.1 24.3 24.6
Matt 14 22.0 21.5 21.4 21.6
;;;;
```

Reading Data from External Files

An external file is managed by your operating system and not by SAS. SAS can read and write many types of external files. Your DATA step code manages the processing of these external files.

If the program above was submitted under Windows and the raw data were stored in the file c:\readdata\runnersapril.dat, the DATA step to read the external file could be written as follows. The INFILE statement identifies the external file containing the raw data.

Example 1.2 Reading Data Lines from an External File

```
data runners;
   infile 'c:\readdata\runnersapril.dat';
   input name $ age runtime1 runtime2 runtime3 runtime4;
run;
```

Understanding Data Values

Once you know the structure of the data value that you want to read or write, you must define to SAS whether your data value is numeric or character and you must determine the method that you want SAS to use to process that value. The coding of your DATA step statements requires that you understand the type of data you are processing. Instructions may also be needed to tell SAS how your data values are represented. Informats and formats provide this information.

A numeric data value represents a number. This value may be simply numbers or it may include characters such as a decimal point or a minus sign. A value written in scientific notation is also considered a numeric data value.

A character data value contains a character or sequence of characters. These characters can be letters, numbers, or symbols.

Guidelines for defining numeric data and character data are fully described in *SAS Language Reference: Concepts*, and *SAS Language Reference: Dictionary*.

SAS defines two styles of representing raw data: standard and nonstandard.

Standard data are character or numeric data values that can be read with list, column, formatted, or named input. A number with a decimal point or a preceding minus sign is considered a standard numeric data value as is a value represented in scientific notation.

Nonstandard data include numeric data values that contain nonnumeric characters. Examples include

❐ numbers with dollar signs or commas or both

❐ dates and times

❐ packed decimal and integer binary numbers.

Character data that is considered nonstandard would include data that was stored in EBCDIC but is being read on an ASCII system.

These values can be read only with informats or written only with formats. Informats translate the nonstandard data into a form that can be processed within SAS. Formats write out data values in a specific form that may be different than the SAS internal representation of the data value.

A date in the form mm/dd/yyyy is a nonstandard data value. To have SAS understand this as a date, you must read the value with an informat. SAS then translates this nonstandard data value to a numeric value—the number of days before or since January 1, 1960. When writing it out, if a format was not used, the date would be represented simply as the number of days before or since January 1, 1960. You need to apply a format to that data value to write it out in a form that is easily understood as a date.

This next example reads payment information. The three variables are payer id and two payment dates. The payment dates are read with formatted input with the MMDDYY10. informat. The PROC PRINT report that follows shows a format applied to PAYDATE1 and not to PAYDATE2. Therefore, the values of PAYDATE2 are presented the way SAS stores them—the number of days since January 1, 1960.

Example 1.3 Working with Dates

```
data payments;
   input id $4.   @6 paydate1 mmddyy10.
                  @17 paydate2 mmddyy10.;
datalines;
QDSW 04/15/2002  06/15/2002
JDHA 5-2-02      8-1-2002
MPWZ 12012002    03042003
;;;;
proc print data=payments;
   title 'Payment Dates';
   format paydate1 mmddyy10.;
run;
```

Output 1.3 PROC PRINT of PAYMENTS Data Set

```
                    Payment Dates
         Obs     id      paydate1     paydate2
          1     QDSW    04/15/2002     15506
          2     JDHA    05/02/2002     15553
          3     MPWZ    12/01/2002     15768
```

SAS language includes many informats and formats that can process different kinds of data. Refer to *SAS Language Reference: Dictionary* for complete specifications.

Reading Raw Data with the INPUT Statement

Your INPUT statement tells SAS how your raw data are structured. There are several different styles of input and you must determine the style that would best read your raw data. Your INPUT statement can be written in a combination of styles.

The four styles of input in SAS are

❐ list input and a hybrid of list and formatted input called modified list input

❐ column input

❐ formatted input

❐ named input.

Following are brief descriptions of the input styles. Complete information on coding your INPUT statements is covered in *SAS Language Reference: Dictionary*. The examples in this book use these input styles to read raw data.

Reading Data Lines with List Input

List input scans your input data lines for data values. Data values do not have to be aligned in columns, but they do have to be separated from one another by a space or other delimiter such as a comma (,). List input requires only that you specify the variable names to be assigned to the data values in your input data line. Unless defined elsewhere in your DATA step, such as in a LENGTH or an ATTRIB statement, a dollar sign ($) must follow the name of a character variable.

The type of data that list input can read is restricted to specific structures. The restrictions are as follows:

❐ Data values must be separated by at least one blank or by another delimiter.

❐ A real placeholder, not a blank, must represent a missing value. A single period (.) denotes the presence of a missing numeric value in your raw data. For data values separated by a delimiter other than a blank, the delimiter serves as a placeholder for the missing value.

❐ Processing character data values greater than the default character length of 8 bytes requires additional specifications. One way to do this is to define the length of the character variable prior to the INPUT statement by using a LENGTH, INFORMAT, or ATTRIB statement. Another way is by using modified list input where a colon and informat follow the character variable name. Modified list input is described later in this chapter.

❐ Specific options must be included if character data values can contain the delimiter.

❐ Fields must be read in the order they appear in the data line, but they do not have to occupy specific columns.

❐ Only standard data values can be read with list input. Use modified list input to read nonstandard data values.

Example 1.1 presents a DATA step that reads data with list input.

Reading Data Lines with Column Input

Column input reads standard data values that are aligned in specific columns in the data lines. The range in columns for a variable follows the variable name. If the variable is character, place a dollar sign between the variable name and the column range. Additional features of column input include the following:

❐ Placeholders for missing values are not required.

❐ Data values can be read in the order you specify; it is not necessary to specify in the INPUT statement the variables in the order they appear in the data lines.

❒ Data values must be in the same columns in all the data lines.

❒ Data values or parts of data values can be reread.

❒ Leading blanks within the field are removed.

❒ Values do not have to be separated by blanks or other delimiters.

❒ Column input can read only standard character and numeric data values.

❒ Character data values can contain embedded delimiters. For example, SAS can read multiple words as one data value.

An example of column input follows. This example demonstrates that columns can be reread.

Example 1.4 Reading Data Lines with Column Input

```
data stores;
   input  storeid $ 1-6 state $ 1-2
          phone 7-16 areacode 7-9
          zipcode 17-25 zip1 17-21 zip2 22-25;
datalines;
WI03819205553945549101234
WI62356085553823537007362
WI72007155554820550017654
WI54124145550087532003221
;;;;
```

PROC PRINT displays the STORES data set.

Output 1.4 PROC
PRINT of STORES Data
Set

```
                    Stores in Wisconsin


Obs  storeid  state     phone    areacode   zipcode   zip1   zip2

1     WI0381   WI     9205553945     920    549101234  54910  1234
2     WI6235   WI     6085553823     608    537007362  53700  7362
3     WI7200   WI     7155554820     715    550017654  55001  7654
4     WI5412   WI     4145550087     414    532003221  53200  3221
```

Reading Data Lines with Formatted Input

Formatted input provides you with the most flexibility when reading data lines. You can read both standard and nonstandard data with formatted input. Pointer controls in the INPUT statement can direct where SAS should read data for a specific variable and informats can specify the structure of the data value. Additional features of formatted input include the following:

❒ Character data values can contain embedded delimiters.

❒ Placeholders for missing values are not required.

❐ Data values can be read in the order you specify; it is not necessary to specify the variables in the order they appear in the data lines. Pointer controls can direct where SAS should read data values.

❐ Data values or parts of data values can be reread.

An example of formatted input follows. The column pointer controls, the at sign (@) and the plus sign (+), specify the position of the column pointer as SAS reads a data line. The number following the @ tells SAS to move to that column. The number following the + tells SAS to move the pointer that number of columns.

Example 1.5 Reading Data Lines with Formatted Input

```
data patients;

 input @1 id $5.


        @1 initials $3. +3 ssn comma11.


        @19 (test1-test3) (4. +1)  ;
datalines;
AFG03 999-99-0393 381  1.3   5
TEY01 999-99-7362            3
REW17 999-99-4313 25   3     0
;;;;
```

Starting in column 1, read a character variable that is five bytes in length. After reading the variable, the pointer is positioned at column 6.

Move the pointer back to column 1 and reread the data in columns 1-3. Move the pointer to the right three columns and read the next variable.

Move the line pointer to column 19. Read the three test values with the 4. informat. Skip one space between each of the test values.

PROC PRINT displays the PATIENTS data set.

Output 1.5 PROC PRINT of PATIENTS Data Set

```
                  Patients in Study

 Obs     id    initials      ssn      test1   test2   test3
  1    AFG03      AFG      999990393    381    1.3       5
  2    TEY01      TEY      999997362     .      .        3
  3    REW17      REW      999994313     25    3.0       0
```

Reading Data Lines with Modified List Input

Modified list input is a hybrid between list input and formatted input. As with simple list input, this style is restricted to reading variables in order. The data values do not have to be aligned in columns, but they do have to be separated from one another by a space or other delimiter such as a comma. Additionally, you can include informats that allow you to read more complex data values than you can read with simple list input. For example, modified list input can read nonstandard numeric data and character data values larger than 8 bytes.

Format modifiers and informats added to the INPUT statement enable you to read more complex data values than you can read with simple list input. The three format modifiers are:

❑ The ampersand (&) format modifier following the variable name tells SAS to read character data values that contain embedded delimiters. SAS stops reading the character data value when it encounters more than one consecutive delimiter.

❑ The colon (:) format modifier and an informat following the variable name tell SAS to read the data value with the informat and to read until it encounters the specified delimiter or reaches the width specified by the informat, whichever comes first.

❑ The tilde (~) format modifier following the variable name tells SAS to treat single quotation marks, double quotation marks, and delimiters within the data value as part of the data value.

An example of a DATA step that uses modified list input follows.

Example 1.6. Reading Data Lines with Modified List Input

```
data survey;

   infile datalines


          delimiter=',';

   input name : $15.


         comments ~ $50.;
datalines;
Mary Ann,More restrictions on emails
Scott,Did not like slogan "Our Team is Tops"
Luke,Would like to have comp time
Rosa,Would like manager's input on reports
;;;;
```

Indicate that raw data is part of the job stream and follows the DATALINES statement.

Specify that commas separate the two fields in the data lines.

Read to the delimiter or read 15 bytes, whichever occurs first.

Read up to 50 bytes. Treat single quotation marks, double quotation marks, and delimiters within the data value as part of the data value.

PROC PRINT displays the SURVEY data set.

Output 1.6 PROC PRINT of SURVEY SAS Data Set

```
                    Survey Results
  Obs    name                      comments
   1     Mary Ann   More restrictions on emails
   2     Scott      Did not like slogan "Our Team is Tops"
   3     Luke       Would like to have comp time
   4     Rosa       Would like manager's input on reports
```

Reading Data Lines with Named Input

Named input requires that the variable name be part of the data line. The variable name followed by an equal sign precedes the data value. Features of named input include:

❑ Named input can be used in combination with other input styles. Once you start named input, you must stay in that style to read the remaining variables.

❑ Only the variables named in the INPUT statement are read. The named variables that exist in data lines but not in the INPUT statement are not included in the output data set. They are, however, identified in the SAS log as not being defined. SAS sets the automatic error variable, _ERROR_, to **1** when named variables appear in the data lines but SAS does not find them in the INPUT statement.

❑ Named input can read only standard data values.

❑ As with simple list input, SAS defaults to assigning the lengths of character variables to 8 bytes. If your character data value is longer than 8 bytes, specify a LENGTH or ATTRIB statement before the INPUT statement.

An example of reading data lines with named input follows. This example demonstrates that only the variables specified in the INPUT statement are written to the output data set.

Example 1.7 Reading Data Lines with Named Input

```
data grades;
```

Since the length of NAME is 15 and greater than the default of 8, place a LENGTH statement before the INPUT statement.

```
  length name $ 15;
```

For named input, follow each variable name with an equal sign (=). If the variable is character, follow the equal sign with a dollar sign ($). Read two of the four variables.

```
  input name=$ math=;
datalines;
name=Linda english=95 math=94 science=90
name=Susan math=88 english=91 science=90
name=Mary Louise math=90 english=84 science=81
;;;;
```

PROC PRINT displays the GRADES data set.

Output 1.7 PROC PRINT of GRADES Data Set

```
            Math Grades
     Obs      name           math
      1       Linda           94
      2       Susan           88
      3       Mary Louise      90
```

A Checklist for Specifying Your External File

SAS follows the instructions you specify in your statements when reading external files. With so much flexibility in the SAS language, you may have to specify several items to successfully read your external file.

The following list presents some of the items you may need to consider when coding your program.

How are the data values arranged in the data lines?

✔ Not column aligned, with delimiters separating the values

✔ Column aligned

What types of data values are you reading?

✔ Character

✔ Numeric

✔ Nonstandard numeric data

How are missing values represented?

✔ Blanks

✔ A character such as a period (.)

✔ A delimiter, if delimiters separate data values

Are the data values fixed or variable in length? If variable, what is the maximum length? If no delimiters separate data values, how do you determine the length of your data value that is variable in length?

How many data lines contain the information for one observation?

✔ One data line per observation

✔ Multiple data lines per observation

✔ Multiple observations per data line

What are the attributes of your external file?

✔ Variable-length records

✔ Fixed-length records

✔ Record length and block size

Are all your data lines structured the same way? Do you need to examine the data line to determine what type of data line it is before you completely read it?

Are all your data lines in one file? Are they in multiple files?

Is your external file on your local system or do you need to connect to a remote system to read the file?

CHAPTER 2
SPECIFYING THE STRUCTURE OF EXTERNAL FILES

Introduction

This chapter illustrates SAS features that assist you in reading external files. There are many different external file structures. The SAS language offers many parameters and options to handle reading the various file structures.

The examples in this chapter focus on INFILE statement options that describe the structure of your external files to SAS. Many of the same options can alternatively be specified in the FILENAME statement. Features of the INPUT statement are also illustrated in this chapter.

The INFILE statement is an executable statement and must be placed in your DATA step ahead of the INPUT statement that reads the external file. You can have multiple INFILE statements in a DATA step, either reading multiple files or reading the same file more than once.

The INFILE statement can directly or indirectly identify an external file. You can identify the external file by explicitly specifying its complete name in the INFILE statement as shown in the next DATA step.

```
data students;
   infile 'c:\readdata\studentsfall2002.dat';
   input studentid 1-8 classnumber1-classnumber5;
run;
```

Alternatively, you can indirectly identify the external file in the INFILE statement with a fileref. The fileref MYFILE in the INFILE statement below points to the file specified in the FILENAME statement that precedes the DATA step.

```
filename myfile 'c:\readdata\studentsfall2002.dat';

data students;
   infile myfile;
   input studentid 1-8 classnumber1-classnumber5;
run;
```

Example Overview

This table presents an overview of the features of the examples in this chapter. All external files in this chapter are structured so that one data line results in one observation.

External File Features	2.1	2.2	2.3	2.4	2.5	2.6	2.7	2.8	2.9	2.10	2.11	2.12	2.13
Data values aligned in columns							●	●	●		●	●	●
Data values not aligned in columns	●	●	●	●	●	●				●			
Data values delimited by a space	●												
Data values delimited by a comma		●		●	●	●				●			
Data values delimited by a character other than a space or comma			●	●									
Delimiter may be part of a data value				●		●							
Fixed length records							●	●	●				
Quotation marks enclose some data values				●		●							
Variable length records	●	●	●	●	●	●				●	●	●	●
Some data values are missing	●				●	●			●			●	●
Some numeric data values are nonstandard						●						●	●
Input Style	**2.1**	**2.2**	**2.3**	**2.4**	**2.5**	**2.6**	**2.7**	**2.8**	**2.9**	**2.10**	**2.11**	**2.12**	**2.13**
List input	●	●	●		●					●			

Input Style	2.1	2.2	2.3	2.4	2.5	2.6	2.7	2.8	2.9	2.10	2.11	2.12	2.13
Column input									●				
Formatted input							●	●			●	●	●
Modified list input				●		●	●			●			
INFILE Statement Features	**2.1**	**2.2**	**2.3**	**2.4**	**2.5**	**2.6**	**2.7**	**2.8**	**2.9**	**2.10**	**2.11**	**2.12**	**2.13**
Specify a character that delimits fields in an external file (DELIMITER=)		●	●	●	●								
Set the default delimiter to a comma, treat two consecutive delimiters as a missing value, and remove quotation marks from character values (DSD)		●		●	●	●					●		
Create a variable that detects when SAS reads the last data line from an external file (END=)							●	●	●	●			
Define a variable that SAS sets to the physical name of the currently opened input file (FILENAME=)										●			
Define a variable whose values determine the input files that the DATA step opens (FILEVAR=)								●	●				
Control how a DATA step executes if an INPUT statement reaches the end of the current input line without finding values for all variables in the INPUT statement (FLOWOVER, MISSOVER, STOPOVER, TRUNCOVER)											●	●	●
Specify the length of the input record (LRECL=)											●		
Control whether SAS pads the data lines that are read from an external file with blanks to the length that is specified in the LRECL= option (PAD | NOPAD)											●		
Other Features	**2.1**	**2.2**	**2.3**	**2.4**	**2.5**	**2.6**	**2.7**	**2.8**	**2.9**	**2.10**	**2.11**	**2.12**	**2.13**
Read from more than one external file in the same DATA Step							●	●	●				
Macro facility										●			

Example 2.1   Reading Space Delimited Data

Goal

Read an external file where the data values are separated by spaces and are not aligned in columns. Some of the data values are missing.

Strategy

Write the INPUT statement in list input style. Identify the external file containing the data values in the INFILE statement.

Example Features

This example reads an external file that has the following features:

❐   Data values are not aligned in columns.

❐   Data values are delimited by a space.

❐   Records have variable lengths.

❐   Some data values are missing.

The style of input used in this example is

❐   list input.

This example does not require any INFILE statement options.

External File

This external file contains expense information for four employes.

```
A03885 HR 1039.65 543.87 109.83 257.45
A03918 Acctg 3029.98 837.00 . 362.91
A05291 . . . . .
A06573 IT 5603.81 2091.23 393.39 103.95
```

The six fields in each data line in order are as follows:

1. person id

2. department

3. hardware expense

4. software expense

5. books expense

6. supplies expense.

The fields are separated by spaces and are not column aligned. A period (.) represents a missing value.

In the third data line, the only information recorded is the person id.

Resulting Data Set

*Output 2.1 PROC
PRINT of EXPENSES
Data Set*

```
                         Expenses by Employee
Obs    personid    dept    hardware   software   books    supplies
1      A03885      HR      1039.65    543.87     109.83   257.45
2      A03918      Acctg   3029.98    837.00     .        362.91
3      A05291      .       .          .    .
4      A06573      IT      5603.81    2091.23    393.39   103.95
```

Program

**Identify the external file in the
INFILE statement.** Do not add
any options to the INFILE
statement since spaces delimit
the data values and the default
delimiter is a space.

Read the data with list input.
Place a dollar sign after the two
variables, PERSONID and
DEPT, since they are character
variables. SAS assigns the
default character variable
length of 8 to these two
variables.

This DATA step reads an external file with list input.

```
data expenses;

infile 'c:\readdata\example2_1.dat';

   input personid $ dept $ hardware software books supplies;
run;
proc print data=expenses;
   title 'Expenses by Employee';
run;
```

A Closer Look

Understanding Lengths of Variables

The INPUT statement in the example reads two character variables
and four numeric variables. The DATA step does not contain any
other statements that define lengths of these variables. Therefore, SAS
assigns the default length of 8 to each of the character variables and to
each of the numeric variables.

To completely read with list input a character data value whose length
is greater than 8, specify the variable's length with a LENGTH or
ATTRIB statement.

For example, if the second data line of this example was modified so that Acctg was replaced by Accounting, the INPUT statement of the example would only read the first 8 characters of the data value.

```
A03885 HR 1039.65 543.87 109.83 257.45
A03918 Accounting 3029.98 837.00 . 362.91
A05291 . . . . .
A06573 IT 5603.81 2091.23 393.39 103.95
```

The value of DEPT for the second observation would be **Accounti**.

Modify the step as follows to ensure that the data values for DEPT are completely read.

```
data expenses;
   infile 'c:\readdata\example2_1.dat';
   length dept $ 10;
   input personid $ dept $ hardware software books supplies;
run;
```

The value of DEPT for the second observation is now **Accounting**.

Example 2.2   Reading Comma Delimited Data

Goal

Read an external file where the data values are separated by commas and are not aligned in columns.

Strategy

Write the INPUT statement in list input style. Include the DELIMITER= option in the INFILE statement and specify a comma as the value for that option.

Example Features

This example reads an external file that has the following features:

❐   Data values are not aligned in columns.

❐   Data values are delimited by a comma.

❐   Records have variable lengths.

❐   No data values are missing.

The style of input used in this example is

❐   list input.

The INFILE statement options described in this example are

❐   DELIMITER= option

❐   DSD option.

External File

This external file contains five data lines. Each data line contains information about one person and the number of books she read.

```
Neda,0,4,0,3,0,11
Amy,8,3,9,2,4,6
Janet,3,0,12,0,2,1
Pauline,0,1,3,0,4,2
Jo Ann,0,1,0,1,0,1
```

The seven fields in each data line in order are as follows:

1.   name

2.   number of biography books read

3.   number of business books read

4.   number of fiction books read

5.   number of science books read

6.   number of self-help books read

7.   number of travel books read.

There are no missing data values.

Resulting Data Set

Output 2.2 PROC PRINT of
BOOKSREAD Data Set

```
                         Number of Books Read
Obs  name  biography  business  fiction  science  selfhelp  travel

1    Neda       0         4         0        3        0        11
2    Amy        8         3         9        2        4         6
3    Janet      3         0        12        0        2         1
4    Pauline    0         1         3        0        4         2
5    Jo Ann     0         1         0        1        0         1
```

Program

This DATA step reads an external file with list input.

```
data booksread;
   infile 'c:\readdata\example2_2.dat'
```

Specify that a comma delimits data values. (Optionally, abbreviate the DELIMITER keyword as DLM.)

```
            delimiter=',';
   input name $ biography business fiction science selfhelp
         travel;
run;
proc print data=booksread;
   title 'Number of Books Read';
run;
```

Related Technique

Another way to indicate that a comma delimits data values is to replace the DELIMITER= option with the DSD option. By default, the DSD option interprets commas as delimiting data values.

The DSD option has additional features. When you include DSD in the INFILE statement, SAS treats two consecutive delimiters as a missing value and removes quotation marks that enclose character values.

When a character other than a comma delimits data values and two consecutive delimiters represent missing data, include both the DELIMITER= option and the DSD option.

The DATA step above is modified below to use the DSD option instead of the DELIMITER= option.

```
data booksread;
   infile 'c:\readdata\example2_2.dat' dsd;
   input name $ biography business fiction science selfhelp
         travel;
run;
```

Where to Go From Here

Example 2.3 presents an example of using the DELIMITER= option where the delimiter is not a comma.

Example 2.3   Reading Tab Delimited Data

Goal

Read an external file where the data values are separated by tabs and are not aligned in columns.

Strategy

Write the INPUT statement in list input style. Include the DELIMITER= option in the INFILE statement. Determine the hexadecimal value of the tab on your operating system and specify that as the value of the DELIMITER= option

Example Features

This example reads an external file that has the following features:

❑ Data values are not aligned in columns.

❑ Data values are delimited by the tab character.

❑ Records have variable lengths.

❑ No data values are missing.

The style of input used in this example is

❑ list input.

The INFILE statement option described in this example is the

❑ DELIMITER= option.

External File

This external file contains six data lines. Each data line represents the number of calls of different types that a computer help line consultant received.

```
Pat^12^0^30^10^25
Louise^22^16^45^38^67
Howard^43^88^0^0^103
Terri^8^70^5^1^10
Martin^21^10^3^0^33
Billy^9^0^18^19^14
```

Assume that the caret symbol (^) in the data lines above represents a tab.

The six fields in each data line in order are as follows:

1. name of computer help line consultant

2. number of calls about passwords

3. number of calls about hardware

4. number of calls about word processing programs

5. number of calls about spreadsheet programs

6. number of calls about computer viruses.

There are no missing data values.

Resulting Data Set

Output 2.3 PROC PRINT of
HELPLINE Data Set

```
         Number of Help Line Calls by Consultant
Obs   name    password  hardware  wordproc  spreadsheet  virus
1     Pat        12         0        30          10        25
2     Louise     22        16        45          38        67
3     Howard     43        88         0           0       103
4     Terri       8        70         5           1        10
5     Martin     21        10         3           0        33
6     Billy       9         0        18          19        14
```

Program

This DATA step reads an external file with list input.

This program executes on an ASCII system so the hexadecimal value of the tab character is `'09'x`. (On an EBCDIC system, such as OS/390, the hexadecimal value of the tab character is `'05'x`.)

```
data helpline;
   infile 'c:\readdata\example2_3.dat'
          delimiter='09'x;
   input name $ password hardware wordproc spreadsheet
         virus;
run;
proc print data=helpline;
   title 'Number of Help Line Calls by Consultant';
run;
```

Example 2.4 Reading Delimited Data Where the Delimiter May Be Part of the Data

Goal

Read an external file where the data values may contain the character that separates the data values. The data values are enclosed in quotation marks and are not aligned in columns. Some of the character data values are greater than 8 bytes in length.

Strategy

Write the INPUT statement in the modified list input style. In the INFILE statement identifying the external file, add the DSD option to indicate that a comma separates data values and that any quotation marks surrounding a data value should be removed.

Example Features

This example reads an external file that has the following features:

❐ Data values are not aligned in columns.

❐ Data values are delimited by a comma.

❐ Delimiters may be part of a data value.

❐ Quotation marks enclose data values.

❐ Records have variable lengths.

❐ No data values are missing.

The style of input used in this example is

❐ modified list input.

The INFILE statement options described in this example are the

❐ DELIMITER= option

❐ DSD option.

External File

The data lines in this external file contain the names and addresses for three people.

```
"Reynolds, Randy","3005 Mountain Rd","Germantown,PA 16240"
"Bain, Darlene","Box 44","Springs, WV 25045"
"Board, Carl","Route 44, Box 365","N. Freedom, PA 27460"
```

The fields in the external file in order are as follows:

1. name

2. address line 1

3. address line 2

Each data value is enclosed in quotation marks. Commas separate the data values and may also be part of the data value. There are no missing data values.

Resulting Data Set

*Output 2.4 PROC PRINT of
INFO Data Set*

```
                        Names and Addresses                              1
Obs  name                 address1               address2
1    Reynolds, Randy      3005 Mountain Rd       Germantown,PA 16240
2    Bain, Darlene        Box 44                 Springs, WV 25045
3    Board, Carl          Route 44, Box 365      N. Freedom, PA 27460
```

Program

This DATA step reads an external file with modified list input.

```
data info;
  infile 'c:\readdata\example2_4.dat'


              dsd;



  input name     : $20.
        address1 : $25.
        address2 : $25.;
run;
proc print data=info;
  title "Names and Addresses";
run;
```

🔍 **Indicate that a comma
separates data values and that
quotation marks enclosing a
data value should be removed.**

🔍 **Write the INPUT statement in
modified list input style since
the data values are not aligned
in columns and the character
data values may be greater than
8 bytes.** Place a colon after each
variable name and follow that
with the appropriate informat.
Specify the width of the
informats as the lengths of the
variables.

🔍 **A Closer Look**

Distinguishing Between the DSD and DELIMITER= Options

Unlike Example 2.2, you cannot replace the DSD option with the
DELIMITER= option in this example's DATA step. You must include
the DSD option in this example to indicate that your delimiters may
be embedded in the data values and that quotation marks may enclose
data values.

If you execute the DATA step without the DSD option and with the
DELIMITER=',' option, the commas embedded within the data
values serve as delimiters and SAS does not read your data values the
way you intend.

When you omit DSD, the variables and their values for the first data
line would be:

NAME= "Reynolds

ADDRESS1=Randy"

ADDRESS2="3005 Mountain Rd"

SAS ignores the remaining information in the data line.

If your delimiter is not a comma, you must include both the DSD option and the DELIMITER= option. For example, if your delimiter is the pound sign (#) and the pound sign may be embedded in a data value, write the INFILE statement as follows:

```
infile 'c:\readdata\example2_4.dat' dsd
       delimiter='#';
```

Understanding Format Modifiers

The DATA step above uses the colon (:) format modifier to read the data values. There are two other format modifiers in addition to the colon. These format modifiers enable you to read complex character values with modified list input. Often these modifiers control inclusion and exclusion of quotation marks and delimiters within a data value.

The following table describes the three format modifiers.

Format Modifier	Description
Ampersand (&)	Read character data values that contain single embedded blanks. If the delimiter is a space, ensure that at least two consecutive blanks separate data values. Place the ampersand between the variable name and the informat. (Remember to leave a space between the ampersand and the informat to prevent SAS from interpreting the informat as a macro variable.)
Colon (:)	Read the data value with the informat that follows the colon (:) and read it until SAS encounters the specified delimiter or the length specified by the informat, whichever comes first. Place the colon between the variable name and the informat.
Tilde (~)	Treat single quotation marks, double quotation marks, and delimiters within the data value as part of the data value. Place the tilde before the variable name.

Another way to store this external file follows. This new file includes the same three fields, but quotation marks no longer enclose the data values and two spaces separate the data values. The delimiter between data values is a space, but a space can also be part of a data value.

```
Reynolds, Randy  3005 Mountain Rd  Germantown,PA 16240
Bain, Darlene  Box 44   Springs WV 25045
Board, Carl  Route 44 Box 365  N. Freedom, PA 27460
```

The following DATA step reads this external file correctly and the data set INFO created here is identical to that shown in Output 2.4.

```
data info;
   infile 'c:\readdata\example2_4a.dat';
   input name      & $20.
         address1  & $25.
         address2  & $25.;
run;
```

The DSD option is not needed in this step. With the ampersand format modifier added to the INPUT statement, SAS treats single embedded blanks as part of a data value. At least two consecutive blanks must separate data values.

Where to Go From Here

Refer to Example 2.6 for another example of using format modifiers.

Example 2.5   Reading Missing Data Values When the Values Are Not Aligned in Columns

Goal

Read an external file where some data values are missing and where the data values are not aligned in columns. A comma separates data values in this external file. Two consecutive commas indicate a missing value.

Strategy

Write the INPUT statement in list input style. Include the DSD option in the INFILE statement that identifies the external file.

Example Features

This example reads an external file that has the following features:

❐ Data values are not aligned in columns.

❐ Data values are delimited by a comma.

❐ Records have variable lengths.

❐ Some data values are missing.

The style of input used in this example is

❐ list input.

The INFILE statement options described in this example are the

❐ DELIMITER= option

❐ DSD option.

External File

This external file contains four data lines. Each data line represents one person's responses to a survey.

```
email,13,,,,3,5,2,2,4,,
phone,31,5,,3,3,4,1,,,3,5
phone,46,5,,3,3,4,1,,,3,5
email,63,5,4,5,4,4,4,4,4,5,
```

The twelve fields in order are

1. type of response

2. survey id

3. responses to 10 questions.

Commas separate the data values and the data values are not aligned in columns.

Each data line contains missing values. In the first and fourth data lines the value for question 10, the last question of the survey, is missing.

Resulting Data Set

Output 2.5a PROC PRINT of SURVEY Data Set

```
                          Survey Responses                              1

Obs     type      id   q1   q2   q3   q4   q5   q6   q7   q8   q9   q10

 1      email     13    .    .    .    3    5    2    2    4    .    .
 2      phone     31    5    .    3    3    4    1    .    .    3    5
 3      phone     46    5    .    3    3    4    1    .    .    3    5
 4      email     63    5    4    5    4    4    4    4    4    5    .
```

Program

This DATA step reads an external file with list input.

```
data survey;
   infile 'c:\readdata\example2_5.dat'
          dsd;
```

🔎 **Indicate that commas separate data values and that two consecutive commas specify a missing value.**

Read the data with list input.

```
   input type $ id q1-q10;
run;
proc print data=survey;
   title 'Survey Responses';
run;
```

🔎 A Closer Look

Understanding Delimiters When a Data Value Is Missing

A delimiter holds the place of a data value if the data value is missing. This is true even if the last data value in a data line is missing.

If you omit the last comma in the fourth data line of this example's external file, the program executes with an error and SAS writes the following note to the SAS log.

```
NOTE: LOST CARD.
type=email id=63 q1=5 q2=4 q3=5 q4=4 q5=4 q6=4 q7=4
q8=4 q9=5 q10=. _ERROR_=1 _N_=4
```

The DATA step outputs only the first three observations to the SURVEY data set because it could not successfully find data for the fourth observation's tenth survey question. Without other options specified, the default action of SAS is to move to the next data line to read data not found in the current data line.

Understanding the DSD Option When Reading Missing Values

If your external file used two consecutive delimiters to represent missing values and you used the DELIMITER= option without the DSD option, your DATA step would not recognize consecutive delimiters as missing values and thus not produce the required results.

The DATA step that follows includes only the DELIMITER= option.

```
data survey;
   infile 'c:\readdata\example2_5.dat' delimiter=',';
   input type $ id q1-q10;
run;
```

If the DSD option were omitted from the first DATA step shown in Example 2.5, as it is in the above DATA step. SAS generates errors and writes only two observations to the SURVEY data set. When reading the first data line, SAS reads the first two variables, TYPE and ID, correctly. A series of commas follows. These are ignored. The value of **3** really corresponds to the response to question 4, but instead SAS assigns that value to question 1. SAS does not find enough data in the current data line for the variables specified in the INPUT statement so it moves to the next data line. The first data value in the second data line is "phone" and SAS reads that as the response to question 6 for the first observation. SAS generates an error because it attempts to make the text "phone" numeric.

The responses for questions 7–10 then are read from the rest of the second data line. SAS then starts reading data for the second observation at the beginning of the third data line.

A PROC PRINT of this data set shows how SAS read the data lines when the DSD opion was omitted.

Resulting Data Set

Output 2.5b PROC PRINT of SURVEY Data Set

```
                         Survey Responses

Obs    type     id   q1   q2   q3   q4   q5   q6   q7   q8   q9   q10

 1     email    13   3    5    2    2    4    .    31   5    3    3
 2     phone    46   5    3    3    4    1    3    5    .    63   5
```

Where to Go From Here

The FLOWOVER, MISSOVER, STOPOVER, and TRUNCOVER options control when SAS moves to a new data line to read data for the current observation. Examples 2.11, 2.12, and 2.13 apply these options.

Example 2.6   Reading Nonstandard Data Values That Are Not Aligned in Columns

Goal

Read an external file where the data values are not aligned in columns and are separated by commas. Some of the numeric values contain nonstandard values and require the use of informats to read them. A nonstandard numeric data value contains nonnumeric characters.

Strategy

In the INFILE statement identifying the external file, add the DSD option to indicate that a comma separates data values and that quotation marks surrounding a data value should be removed.

Write the INPUT statement in the modified list input style. Use a colon modifier and the appropriate informat to read each variable.

Assign lengths to the character variables whose lengths are greater than the SAS default length of 8 bytes by specifying the length as the width of the informat. Alternatively, define the lengths of the character variables with an ATTRIB or LENGTH statement that is placed before the INPUT statement. These character variables could then be read with list input instead of modified list input.

Example Features

This example reads an external file that has the following features:

❑ Data values are not aligned in columns.

❑ Data values are delimited by a comma.

❑ Delimiter may be part of a data value.

❑ Quotation marks enclose some data values.

❑ Records have variable lengths.

❑ Some data values are missing.

❑ Some numeric data values are nonstandard.

The style of input used in this example is

❑ modified list input.

The INFILE statement option described in this example is the

❑ DSD option.

External File

This external file contains seven data lines, one for each of the employees hired in 2002.

```
Franklin,Terry,01/15/2002,Sales,"$55,039.39",10%
Yen,Steve,010102,Accounting,"$51,003.00",
Drake,Wanda,02/15/02,Support Staff,"$43,429.37",
Top,Ronald,06/18/2002,Accounting,"$53,387.93",
McFarlen,Virginia,03/01/2002,Design,"$66,938.34",
Robertson,Jonathon,11/15/2002,Design,"$68,382.34",
Marks,Ann Marie,12/01/2002,Sales,"$57,543.00",10%
```

The fields in order in each data line are

1. last name

2. first name

3. date of hire

4. department

5. salary

6. commission percent.

Only the first and last data lines contain a value for commission percent. A single comma at the end of the data line followed by no data indicates that the commission percent is missing.

The quotation marks surrounding a salary value prevents SAS from interpreting the comma in the salary value as a delimiter.

Resulting Data Set

Output 2.6 PROC PRINT of NEWHIRES Data Set

```
                         Employees Hired in 2002


                                         d                       c
                 f                       e                       o
      l          i             h p                               m
      a          r             i a                               m
      s          s             r r                     S         i
      t          t             e t                     a         s
      n          n             d m                     l         s
 O a             a             a e                     a         i
 b m             m             t n                     r         o
 s e             e             e t                     y         n


 1 Franklin     Terry      01/15/2002  Sales          $55,039.39    10%
 2 Yen          Steve      01/01/2002  Accounting     $51,003.00     0%
 3 Drake        Wanda      02/15/2002  Support Staff  $43,429.37     0%
 4 Top          Ronald     06/18/2002  Accounting     $53,387.93     0%
 5 McFarlen     Virginia   03/01/2002  Design         $66,938.34     0%
 6 Robertson    Jonathon   11/15/2002  Design         $68,382.34     0%
 7 Marks        Ann Marie  12/01/2002  Sales          $57,543.00    10%
```

Program

This DATA step reads an external file where the data values are not aligned in columns and where some of the data values are nonstandard numeric values.

Indicate that commas separate the data values, quotation marks enclosing data values should be removed, and two consecutive commas identify a missing value .

Read the data with modified list input. Follow the variable name with the colon format modifer and then the informat. Override the default length of 8 bytes for a character variable by specifying the length of the variable as the width of the informat.

Assign 0 as the value for COMMISSION for the five observations without a commission value.

Format selected variables.

```
data newhires;
  infile 'c:\readdata\example2_6.dat'
         dsd;


  input lastname    : $25.
        firstname   : $15.
        hiredate    : mmddyy10.
        department  : $15.
        salary      : comma11.2
        commission  : percent4.;


  if commission=. then commission=0;


  format hiredate    mmddyy10.
         salary      dollar11.2
         commission  percent5.;
run;
proc print data=newhires;
  title 'Employees Hired in 2002';
run;
```

A Closer Look

Verifying the Length of Variables in a SAS Data Set

The column properties window shows the length of the variables in the NEWHIRES SAS data set.

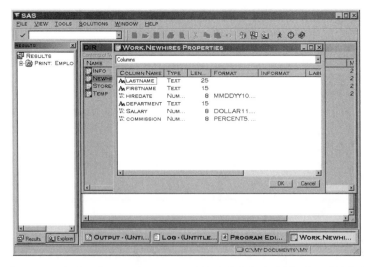

In a nonwindowing environment, PROC CONTENTS or PROC DATASETS can show attribute values for variables in the new data set.

Example 2.7   Reading Multiple External Files

Goal

Read several external files in one DATA step. These external files have the same structure.

Strategy

Write an INFILE statement, a DO UNTIL loop, an INPUT statement, and an OUTPUT statement for each external file that should be read. Include the END= option on each INFILE statement. Test the value of the variable defined with the END= option on the DO UNTIL statement. Write the test so that the loop stops when the last data line from the currently opened external file has been read.

Example Features

This example reads an external file that has the following features:

❐ Data values are aligned in columns.

❐ Records have fixed lengths.

❐ No data values are missing.

The style of input used in this example is

❐ formatted input.

The INFILE statement option described in this example is the

❐ END= option.

This example also shows how to

❐ read from more than one external file in the same DATA Step.

External Files

The three external files contain sales information for several departments. Each file contains information for a specific month and year.

This is the file for January 2003.

01/03	Sporting Goods	18000	15000
01/03	Hardware	35300	38000
01/03	Domestics	25000	32000
01/03	Toys	15000	17735
01/03	Health and Beauty	20000	22000

This is the file for February 2003.

02/03	Sporting Goods	20000	19000
02/03	Hardware	45300	40000
02/03	Domestics	15000	21000
02/03	Toys	25000	23000
02/03	Health and Beauty	22000	22500

This is the file for March 2003.

```
03/03    Sporting Goods              25000        27000
03/03    Hardware                    38600        41000
03/03    Domestics                   18000        17000
03/03    Toys                        26000        25000
03/03    Health and Beauty           26000        21000
```

The data lines in each of the three files have the same structure. The data values are aligned in columns and the layout follows.

Field	Column Range
Month and Year	1–5
Department	9–28
Actual Sales	34–38
Sales Goal	48–52

There are no missing data values.

Resulting Data Set

Output 2.7a PROC PRINT of SALESPERDEPT Data Set

```
                         Sales per Department

    Obs    monyr   department           actualsales      salesgoal

     1     01/03   Sporting Goods       $18,000.00      $15,000.00
     2     01/03   Hardware             $35,300.00      $38,000.00
     3     01/03   Domestics            $25,000.00      $32,000.00
     4     01/03   Toys                 $15,000.00      $17,735.00
     5     01/03   Health and Beauty    $20,000.00      $22,000.00
     6     02/03   Sporting Goods       $20,000.00      $19,000.00
     7     02/03   Hardware             $45,300.00      $40,000.00
     8     02/03   Domestics            $15,000.00      $21,000.00
     9     02/03   Toys                 $25,000.00      $23,000.00
    10     02/03   Health and Beauty    $22,000.00      $22,500.00
    11     03/03   Sporting Goods       $25,000.00      $27,000.00
    12     03/03   Hardware             $38,600.00      $41,000.00
    13     03/03   Domestics            $18,000.00      $17,000.00
    14     03/03   Toys                 $26,000.00      $25,000.00
    15     03/03   Health and Beauty    $26,000.00      $21,000.00
```

Program

This DATA step reads three external files, one at a time.

```
data salesperdept;
```

Identify the first external file.

```
   infile 'c:\readdata\jan2003_2_7.dat'
```

Define a variable that SAS sets to 1 when it reads the last data line in this first external file.

```
          end=endjan;
```

Read the entire January sales external file.

```
   do until (endjan);
```

Read the data with formatted input.

```
     input @1  monyr $5.
           @9  department $20.
           @34 actualsales
           @48 salesgoal;
```

Write each observation created in this loop to the output data set.

```
     output;
   end;
```

Identify the second external file.

```
   infile 'c:\readdata\feb2003_2_7.dat'
```

Define a variable that SAS sets to 1 when it reads the last data line in the second external file.

```
          end=endfeb;
```

Read the entire February sales external file.

```
   do until (endfeb);
```

Read the data with formatted input.

```
     input @1  monyr $5.
           @8  department $20.
           @34 actualsales
           @48 salesgoal;
```

Write each observation created in this loop to the output data set.

```
     output;
   end;
```

Identify the third external file.

```
   infile 'c:\readdata\mar2003_2_7.dat'
```

Define a variable that SAS sets to 1 when it reads the last data line in the third external file.

```
          end=endmar;
```

Read the entire March sales external file.

Read the data with formatted input.

🔍 **Write each observation created in this loop to the output data set.**

```
do until (endmar);


   input @1   monyr $5.
         @9   department $20.
         @34  actualsales
         @48  salesgoal;
   output;
end;


   format actualsales salesgoal dollar10.2;
run;
proc print data=salesperdept;
   title "Sales per Department";
run;
```

🔍 **A Closer Look**

Determining When SAS Writes an Observation to a Data Set

By default, when your DATA step does not include at least one OUTPUT statement, SAS writes an observation to the data set at the bottom of the DATA step at the end of an iteration of the DATA step. If your code does not cause the current iteration to stop before the end of the DATA step, SAS writes the current observation to the data set. You could consider that SAS has an implicit OUTPUT statement at the end of such a DATA step.

Placing an OUTPUT statement in a DATA step overrides the automatic output at the end of the iteration of the DATA step. The DATA step now only writes an observation to a data set when an OUTPUT statement executes.

Understanding How This Data Step Executes

The DATA step in this example iterates twice and it includes three OUTPUT statements. It writes an observation to SALESPERDEPT only when an OUTPUT statement executes. The values of the END= variables control the DO WHILE loops that contain the INPUT and OUTPUT statements.

On the first iteration of the DATA step above, SAS reads all the data lines from the three external files and outputs to SALESPERDEPT the observations created from the external files. On the second iteration, SAS does not read any data values from the external files and it does not write any observations to SALESPERDEPT.

SAS automatically retains the values of the three END= variables across iterations of the DATA step. On the second iteration of the DATA step, the DO WHILE loops do not execute since the values of the END= variables are already 1. The OUTPUT statements thus never execute in the second iteration and SAS does not write any additional observations to SALESPERDEPT.

If you made the END= variable the same in the three INFILE statements, SAS would only write the data lines from the January sales file to SALESPERDEPT. The second and third DO WHILE statements detect that the END= variable is already **1**, so no statements within the second and third loops would execute.

If you omitted the OUTPUT statements in the DO WHILE loops, SALESPERDEPT would contain two observations. The first observation would be the result of the first iteration of the DATA step. This observation would contain the data from the last data line in the third external file, which is the Health and Beauty sales for March. The second observation contains missing values for all variables and represents the processing of the second iteration.

Related Technique

Since the external files in this example have the same structure, you can modify the program by putting the DO WHILE loop in a block that can be linked to for each external file. The DO WHILE loop and the INPUT statement only have to be coded once.

The END= option is set to the same variable, ENDFILE, and the DO WHILE statement tests the value of ENDFILE. When SAS reaches the end of the external file, it sets ENDFILE to **1**. A statement resetting ENDFILE to **0** is placed before the DO WHILE statement. Without resetting ENDFILE to **0**, SAS would not read the second and third external files.

```
data salesperdept;
```

Identify the first external file.
```
   infile 'c:\readdata\jan2003_2_7.dat'
```

Define a variable that SAS sets to 1 when it reads the last data line in this first external file.
```
          end=endfile;
```

Link to the block of code labelled READIT.
```
   link readit;
```

Identify the second external file.
```
   infile 'c:\readdata\feb2003_2_7.dat'
```

Define a variable that SAS sets to 1 when it reads the last data line in this second external file. Use the same name as specified in the first INFILE statement.
```
          end=endfile;
```

Link to the block of code labelled READIT.
```
   link readit;
```

Identify the third external file.
```
   infile 'c:\readdata\mar2003_2_7.dat'
```

Define a variable that SAS sets to 1 when it reads the last data line in this third external file. Use the same name as specified in the first INFILE statement.

```
                 end=endfile;
```

Link to the block of code labelled READIT.

```
  link readit;
```

```
  format actualsales salesgoal dollar10.2;
```

Terminate the main part of the DATA step.

```
return;
```

Read an external file. Label this section on READIT.

```
readit:
```

Set ENDFILE to 0 before executing the DO WHILE statement.

```
  endfile=0;
  do while (not endfile);
```

Read the data with formatted input.

```
  input @1   monyr $5.
        @8   department $20.
        @34 actualsales
        @48 salesgoal;
    output;
  end;
```

Write each observation created in this loop to the output data set.

Terminate the READIT block with the RETURN statement.

```
return;
run;
```

Related Technique

Warning: Do not use this method if the external files have different number of data lines since your results may be incorrect.

The following DATA step creates the SALESPERDEPT data set from the three external files. It includes an INFILE and an INPUT statement for each of the external files. It does not, however, control the reading of the external files with a DO WHILE loop.

This DATA step iterates multiple times. With each iteration, one data line is read from each of the three external files. All external files are opened in the first iteration of the DATA step. They remain open until an end-of-file is reached in the shortest file. Processing of the DATA step then stops. The maximum number of data lines read from any of the files is equal to the number of data lines in the shortest file.

This DATA step executes correctly in this example since the three external files contain the same number of data lines.

```
data salesperdept;
  infile 'c:\readdata\jan2003_2_7.dat';
  input @1   monyr $5.
        @8   department $20.
        @34 actualsales
        @48 salesgoal;
  output;
```

```
        infile 'c:\readdata\feb2003_2_7.dat';
        input @1   monyr $5.
              @8   department $20.
              @34 actualsales
              @48 salesgoal;
        output;

        infile 'c:\readdata\mar2003_2_7.dat';
        input @1   monyr $5.
              @9   department $20.
              @34 actualsales
              @48 salesgoal;
        output;

        format actualsales salesgoal dollar10.2;
    run;
```

In the previous two examples in this section, SAS wrote the observations to SALESPERDEPT in month order because it completely read all the data in one external file before opening the next.

In this third example, SAS writes the observations to SALESPERDEPT in department order. Executing a PROC PRINT step immediately after the DATA step terminates shows the order the data lines were read.

Resulting Data Set

Output 2.7b PROC PRINT of SALESPERDEPT Data Set

```
                        Sales per Department

    Obs    monyr    department           actualsales     salesgoal

     1     01/01    Sporting Goods       $18,000.00     $15,000.00
     2     02/01    Sporting Goods       $20,000.00     $19,000.00
     3     03/01    Sporting Goods       $25,000.00     $27,000.00
     4     01/01    Hardware             $35,300.00     $38,000.00
     5     02/01    Hardware             $45,300.00     $40,000.00
     6     03/01    Hardware             $38,600.00     $41,000.00
     7     01/01    Domestics            $25,000.00     $32,000.00
     8     02/01    Domestics            $15,000.00     $21,000.00
     9     03/01    Domestics            $18,000.00     $17,000.00
    10     01/01    Toys                 $15,000.00     $17,735.00
    11     02/01    Toys                 $25,000.00     $23,000.00
    12     03/01    Toys                 $26,000.00     $25,000.00
    13     01/01    Health and Beauty    $20,000.00     $22,000.00
    14     02/01    Health and Beauty    $22,000.00     $22,500.00
    15     03/01    Health and Beauty    $26,000.00     $21,000.00
```

As with the other examples in this section, an OUTPUT statement follows each INPUT statement.

If you omitted the OUTPUT statements in the above DATA step, SAS would write to SALESPERDEPT only the observations created from the third external file; an implied automatic OUTPUT statement would exist at the end of the DATA step.

Since the same variables are read from each of the external files, the variable values in the second file would overwrite the variable values from the first file. The variable values in the third file would overwrite the variable values from the second file. No other changes are made to the variable values after SAS reads a data line from the third file, so these are the values SAS writes to SALESPERDEPT.

Example 2.8 Reading Multiple External Files Where the Names of the External Files Are Stored in Another External File

Goal

Read several external files in one DATA step. The external files have the same structure. Another external file contains a list of the complete names of the external files that contain the data. Read the list of filenames in the same DATA step that reads the data.

Strategy

Write a DATA step so that during each iteration of the step, SAS reads a filename from the list of filenames and then reads the entire contents of the external file identified by the filename.

Specify an INFILE statement for the external file containing the list of filenames. Read from the list the name of an external file.

Specify a second INFILE statement that identifies the external file containing the data. Include the FILEVAR= option on this statement. Set the option's value to the variable that holds the name of the external file, which was read by the first INPUT statement. Add the END= option to the INFILE statement to define a variable that SAS sets to **1** when it reads the last data line in an external file.

Write a DO WHILE loop to read the contents of an external file. Place an INPUT statement within the loop. Write the INPUT statement to read the data values from an external file.

Specify that the DO WHILE expression test whether the value of the END= variable is **1**. Execute the loop while the END= variable is **0**.

Include an OUTPUT statement at the bottom of the DO LOOP to create an observation for each data line read.

Example Features

This example reads an external file that has the following features:

❐ Data values are aligned in columns.

❐ Records have fixed length.

❐ No data values are missing.

The styles of input used in this example are

❐ formatted input

❐ modified list input.

The INFILE statement options described in this example are the

❐ END= option

❐ FILEVAR= option.

This example also show how to

❐ read from more than one external file in the same DATA step.

External File

This file contains a list of the names of three external files.

```
c:\readdata\jan2003_2_7.dat
c:\readdata\feb2003_2_7.dat
c:\readdata\mar2003_2_7.dat
```

The DATA step should read the contents of each of these files.

External Files

The three external files contain sales information for several departments. Each file contains information for a specific month and year.

This is the file for January 2003.

01/03	Sporting Goods	18000	15000
01/03	Hardware	35300	38000
01/03	Domestics	25000	32000
01/03	Toys	15000	17735
01/03	Health and Beauty	20000	22000

This is the file for February 2003.

02/03	Sporting Goods	20000	19000
02/03	Hardware	45300	40000
02/03	Domestics	5000	21000
02/03	Toys	25000	23000
02/03	Health and Beauty	22000	22500

This is the file for March 2003.

03/03	Sporting Goods	25000	27000
03/03	Hardware	38600	41000
03/03	Domestics	18000	17000
03/03	Toys	26000	25000
03/03	Health and Beauty	26000	21000

The data lines in each of the three files have the same structure. The data values are aligned in columns and the layout follows.

Field	Column Range
Month and Year	1–5
Department	9–28
Actual Sales	34–38
Sales Goal	48–52

There are no missing data values.

Resulting Data Sets

Output 2.8 PROC PRINT of
SALESPERDEPT Data Set

```
                          Sales per Department

     Obs   monyr   department          actualsales   salesgoal

       1   01/03   Sporting Goods       $18,000.00   $15,000.00
       2   01/03   Hardware             $35,300.00   $38,000.00
       3   01/03   Domestics            $25,000.00   $32,000.00
       4   01/03   Toys                 $15,000.00   $17,735.00
       5   01/03   Health and Beauty    $20,000.00   $22,000.00
       6   02/03   Sporting Goods       $20,000.00   $19,000.00
       7   02/03   Hardware             $45,300.00   $40,000.00
       8   02/03   Domestics            $15,000.00   $21,000.00
       9   02/03   Toys                 $25,000.00   $23,000.00
      10   02/03   Health and Beauty    $22,000.00   $22,500.00
      11   03/03   Sporting Goods       $25,000.00   $27,000.00
      12   03/03   Hardware             $38,600.00   $41,000.00
      13   03/03   Domestics            $18,000.00   $17,000.00
      14   03/03   Toys                 $26,000.00   $25,000.00
      15   03/03   Health and Beauty    $26,000.00   $21,000.00
```

Program

This DATA step reads several external files in one DATA step. The names of the external files are stored in another external file. This DATA step reads the list to determine the external files it should read.

```
data salesperdept;
   infile 'c:\readdata\salesfiles_2_7.dat';
```

Specify the name of the external file containing the list of filenames that the DATA step should read.

Read the name of the external file with modified list input. Specify a width sufficient to hold the name of the external file.

```
   input salesfile : $75.;
```

Specify the text, dummy, as a placeholder for the required file-specification on the INFILE statement. (The actual specification for the input file comes from the value of the variable assigned by the FILEVAR= option.)

```
   infile dummy
```

Set the FILEVAR= option to SALESFILE, the variable that contains the name of the external file that the current iteration of the DATA step should read.

```
filevar=salesfile
```

Define a variable that SAS sets to 1 when it reads the last data line in the currently opened external file.

```
end=endfile;
```

Read all the data lines in the external file specified by the FILEVAR= option. Control the DO WHILE loop by testing the value of the END= variable. Write the expression so that the loop stops after SAS reads the last data line in the currently opened external file.

```
do while (not endfile);
  input @1  monyr $5.
        @8  department $20.
        @34 actualsales
        @48 salesgoal;
```

Write each observation to the output data set.

```
    output;
  end;
  format actualsales salesgoal dollar10.2;
run;
proc print data=salesperdept;
  title "Sales per Department";
run;
```

A Closer Look

Understanding How the FILEVAR= Option Controls the Value of the END= Variable

When you include the FILEVAR= option on the INFILE statement, SAS resets the END= variable to **0** when the value of the FILEVAR= variable changes.

SAS initializes to **0** the variable you name with the END= option on the INFILE statement. SAS retains the value of the END= variable as **0** until it detects that the current input data line is the last in the external file referenced by the INFILE statement. SAS then sets the variable to **1**.

This example reads multiple external files. Each time the INFILE statement in this example executes, it references a different external file. This file is identified by the value of the FILEVAR= variable, SALESFILE. Each time a new external file is opened, SAS resets the END= variable, ENDFILE, to **0**.

If SAS did not reset the value of the END= variable to **0** each time it opened a new external file, the DATA step would stop after reading the first external file. You would then have to specify code to set the END= variable to **0**.

Understanding How This DATA Step Outputs Observations

This DATA step iterates four times: once for each of the sales files and a fourth time in which it detects that there are no more data lines in the external file that contains the filenames.

If you omitted the OUTPUT statement in the DO WHILE loop, SALESPERDEPT would contain just three observations, the Health and Beauty sales for each of the three months.

By default, when an OUTPUT statement is not present in a DATA step, SAS automatically writes an observation to a data set only at the end of each iteration of the DATA step.

Related Technique

The following example presents a DATA step where the names of the external files that should be read are stored in a SAS data set instead of an external file. This DATA step iterates the number of times equal to the number of observations in the WORK.EXTFILES data set.

```
data salesperdept;
   set extfiles;
```

Follow the DATA statement with a SET statement that identifies the data set that contains the names of the external files. Assume that SALESFILE is the variable that holds the names.

Write the remainder of the DATA step as was shown in the previous DATA step.

```
   infile dummy
          filevar=salesfile
          end=endfile;

   do while (not endfile);
     input @1  monyr $5.
           @8  department $20.
           @34 actualsales
           @48 salesgoal;
     output;
   end;
   format actualsales salesgoal dollar10.2;
run;
```

Where to Go From Here

Refer to the technical support document, TS-581 "Using FILEVAR= to Read Multiple External Files in a DATA Step" for more information on applying the FILEVAR= option.

Example 2.9   Reading from Multiple External Files and Determining the Names of the External Files within the DATA Step

Goal

Read several external files in one DATA step. These external files have the same structure. Derive complete names of the external files within the DATA step.

Strategy

Write an iterative DO loop that iterates the number of times equal to the number of external files that should be read. Include an INFILE statement within this loop.

Based on information known about the external files, define a variable that holds the complete name of the external file. Specify this variable as the value of the FILEVAR= option of the INFILE statement.

Add the END= option to the INFILE statement to define a variable that SAS sets to **1** when it reads the last data line in an external file.

Within the iterative DO loop, write a DO WHILE loop that reads all the data lines from the currently opened external file. Specify that the DO WHILE expression test whether the value of the END= variable is **1**. Execute the loop while the END= variable is **0**.

Place within the DO WHILE loop the INPUT statement that reads the data lines from the external file.

Place an OUTPUT statement at the bottom of the DO WHILE loop to write observations to the data set.

Example Features

This example reads an external file that has the following features:

❒   Data values aligned in columns.

❒   Records have fixed lengths.

❒   Some data values are missing.

The style of input used in this example is

❒   column input.

The INFILE statement options described in this example are the

❒   END= option

❒   FILEVAR= option.

This example also shows how to

❒   read from more than one external file in the same DATA step.

External Files

The four external files read in this example contain grades for four students for four quarters.

This is the QTR1.DAT file.

Dana	98	96	96	98
Charley	80	84	88	80
Martin	78	74	80	100
Amber	100	84	.	96

This is the QTR2.DAT file.

Dana	98	96	96	98
Charley	80	84	88	80
Martin	78	74	80	100
Amber	90	82	88	98

This is the QTR3.DAT file.

Dana	64	72	80	76
Charley	80	84	88	92
Martin	.	100	100	100
Amber	88	86	84	70

This is the QTR4.DAT file.

Dana	98	92	90	99
Martin	70	80	90	100
Amber	90	90	90	90

The data values are aligned in columns and are in the following order:

1. student name

2. chemistry grade

3. English grade

4. history grade

5. mathematics grade.

Grades exist for four students in the first three quarters. In the fourth quarter file, grades exist for only three students.

Resulting Data Set

Output 2.9 PROC PRINT of GRADES Data Set

```
                        Quarterly Test Scores

    Obs   quarter   name     chemistry   english   history   mathematics

     1       1      Dana         98         96        96          98
     2       1      Charley      80         84        88          80
     3       1      Martin       78         74        80         100
     4       1      Amber       100         84         .          96
     5       2      Dana         98         96        96          98
     6       2      Charley      80         84        88          80
     7       2      Martin       78         74        80         100
     8       2      Amber        90         82        88          98
     9       3      Dana         64         72        80          76
    10       3      Charley      80         84        88          92
    11       3      Martin        .        100       100         100
    12       3      Amber        88         86        84          70
    13       4      Dana         98         92        90          99
    14       4      Martin       70         80        90         100
    15       4      Amber        90         90        90          90
```

Program

This DATA step reads four external files. The complete names of the external files are determined within the DATA step.

```
data grades;
  do quarter=1 to 4;
```

Read the four external files with a DO loop that iterates four times.

```
    classdata='c:\readdata\qtr' ||
```

Create the variable CLASSDATA to hold the complete name of the external file.

```
                  put(quarter,1.) || '.dat';
```

Use the value of the index variable QUARTER when defining the name of the external file.

```
    infile dummy
```

Specify the text, dummy, as a placeholder for the required file-specification on the INFILE statement.

Set the FILEVAR= option to CLASSDATA, the variable that contains the physical name of the external file.	`filevar=classdata`
Define a variable that SAS sets to 1 when it reads the last data line in the external file.	`end=endfile;`
Read all the data lines in the external file specified by the current value of the FILEVAR= variable, CLASSDATA. Control the DO by testing the value of END= variable.	`do while (not endfile);`

```
      input name        $ 1-12
            chemistry     15-17
            english       20-22
            history       25-27
            mathematics 30-32;
        output;
      end;
    end;

  stop;
run;
```

Read the data with column input.

At the end of each iteration of the DO WHILE loop, write an observation to the output data set.

Prevent the DATA step from executing indefinitely by halting execution of the DATA step. Execute this statement after SAS reads all data files.

🔍 **A Closer Look**

Understanding How This DATA Step Outputs Observations

If you omitted the OUTPUT statement, SAS would not write any observations to GRADES. This DATA step executes once through to the STOP statement. Without an OUTPUT statement, SAS writes data to a data set only at the bottom of the DATA step, at the end of the iteration. Because of the STOP statement, the DATA step never executes to the bottom of the step and SAS thus would not write any observations to GRADES.

Where to Go from Here

Refer to the technical support document, TS-581 "Using FILEVAR= to Read Multiple External Files in a DATA Step" for more information on applying the FILEVAR= option.

Example 2.10   Obtaining the Name of the External File Currently Being Read

Goal

Read an external file where the name of the external file is determined within the DATA step that reads the external file. Place the name of the external file in the title of the report that follows the DATA step.

Strategy

Specify the FILENAME= option in the INFILE statement that identifies the external file. Specify the name of a variable that will hold the name of the external file as the value of the FILENAME= option.

Add the END= option to the INFILE statement. Test the value of the variable defined with the END= option. When the END= variable is **1**, indicating that SAS read the last data line in the file, execute a DO block.

Within the DO block, pass the value of the FILENAME= variable to a macro variable by issuing a call to the SYMPUT routine.

Example Features

This example reads an external file that has the following features:

❏ Data values are not aligned in columns.

❏ Data values are delimited by a comma.

❏ Records have variable lengths.

❏ No data values are missing.

The styles of input used in this example are

❏ list input

❏ modified list input.

The INFILE statement options described in this example are the

❏ DSD option

❏ END= option

❏ FILENAME= option.

Other features of this example include the

❏ macro facility.

External File

This external file contains four data lines. Each data line contains the number of tomatoes of a specific variety in each of four test plots.

```
Brandywine,5,13,0,5
Best Red,8,12,11,13
Roma,15,18,17,8
Chunky Cherry,25,18,30,31
```

The data values are not aligned in columns and are in the following order:

1. tomato variety

2. number of tomatoes in plot 1

3. number of tomatoes in plot 2

4. number of tomatoes in plot 3

5. number of tomatoes in plot 4.

Commas delimit the data values.

Resulting Data Set

Output 2.10 PROC PRINT of VEGGIES Data Set

```
                    Results for tomatoes in 2002              1

    Obs      variety         plot1   plot2   plot3   plot4

     1       Brandywine         5      13       0       5
     2       Best Red           8      12      11      13
     3       Roma              15      18      17       8
     4       Chunky Cherry     25      18      30      31
```

Program

This program reads an external file. A FILENAME statement preceding the DATA step defines the external file that the DATA step reads.

The DATA step creates a macro variable that the program references after the DATA step executes.

Assign a fileref to the external file.

Assign a length to the variable that holds the name of the external file

```
filename plots 'c:\readdata\example2_10.dat';
data veggies(keep=variety plot1-plot4);
  length vegyear $ 100;
```

Reference the fileref defined by the above FILENAME statement.	`infile plots`
Assign the name of the external file to a variable.	`filename=vegyear`
Define a variable that SAS sets to 1 when it reads the last data line in the external file.	`end=lastplot`
Indicate that commas separate the data values.	`dsd;`
Read the character variable VARIETY with modified list input and assign a length of 15 bytes to VARIETY.	`input variety : $15.`
Read the numeric variables, PLOT1, PLOT2, PLOT3, and PLOT4 with list input.	`plot1-plot4;`
Test the value of the END= variable. Execute this DO block only when processing the last data line in the external file.	`if lastplot then do;`
Extract text from the external filename.	`vegyear=scan(vegyear,4,'\');` `vegetable=scan(vegyear,1,'_');`
Create macro variable VEGTITLE with the CALL SYMPUT routine. Apply the LEFT function to the VEGETABLE value in order to left adjust the value. Trim any trailing blanks from VEGETABLE with the TRIM function.	`call symput('vegtitle',trim(left(vegetable)));` `trialyear=scan(vegyear,2,'_');`

Create macro variable YEARTITLE with the CALL SYMPUT routine. Apply the LEFT function to the TRIALYEAR value in order to left adjust the value. Trim any trailing blanks from TRIALYEAR with the TRIM function.	`call symput('yeartitle',trim(left(trialyear)));`
	 `end;`
	 `run;`

Include the macro variables, VEGTITLE and YEARTITLE, in the TITLE statement. Enclose the title in double quotes so that the macro variables resolve and their values appear in the title of the report. (Placing single quotes around the title text prevents resolution of the macro variables.)

```
proc print data=veggies;
   title "Results for &vegtitle in &yeartitle";
run;
```

Related Technique

The SAS function, PATHNAME, can also obtain the name of the external file. This DATA step uses the PATHNAME function instead of the FILENAME= option.

```
filename plots 'c:\readdata\example2_10.dat';

data veggies(keep=variety plot1-plot4);
   length vegyear $ 100;
   infile plots
          end=lastplot
          dsd;

   input variety : $15. plot1-plot4;

   if lastplot then do;
     vegyear=pathname('plots');
     vegyear=scan(vegyear,4,'\');
     vegetable=scan(vegyear,1,'_');
     call symput('vegtitle',trim(left(vegetable)));
     trialyear=scan(vegyear,2,'_');
     call symput('yeartitle',trim(left(trialyear)));
   end;
run;
proc print data=veggies;
   title "Results for &vegtitle in &yeartitle";
run;
```

Omit the FILENAME= option in this revised DATA step. Keep the END= and DSD options as specified in the above example.

Assign to the variable VEGYEAR the complete name of the file associated with the fileref PLOTS.

The PATHNAME function can also be used in conjunction with the %SYSFUNC macro function. The %SYSFUNC macro function can call SAS language functions and assign the results of the SAS language functions to macro variables. In the following revised DATA step, the call to %SYSFUNC executes the PATHNAME function and assigns the name of the external file to the macro variable VEGYEAR.

The open code macro language statements that follow the DATA step replace the SAS language statements that executed when reading the last data line in the DATA step.

Omit the FILENAME= and the END= options in this revised DATA step. Keep the DSD option.

```
filename plots 'c:\readdata\example2_10.dat';
data veggies(keep=variety plot1-plot4);
infile plots
        dsd;

  input variety : $15. plot1-plot4;
run;
```

Determine the name of the external file with the PATHNAME function and place the value obtained by PATHNAME in the macro variable VEGYEAR. Do not place quotation marks around the argument to PATHNAME since the macro language is a text processing language.

```
%let vegyear=%sysfunc(pathname(plots));
%let vegyear=%scan(&vegyear,4,\);
%let vegtitle=%scan(&vegyear,1,_);
%let yeartitle=%scan(&vegyear,2,_);

proc print data=veggies;
    title "Results for &vegtitle in &yeartitle";
run;
```

Example 2.11   Reading Column Aligned Data from Variable Length Data Lines

Goal

Read an external file where the data lines are variable in length and only one data line should be read per observation. The data values are aligned in columns and some data values may not be as long as the INPUT statement expects. If a data value is not as long as expected, assign what is available to the variable being read.

Strategy

Add the TRUNCOVER option to the INFILE statement that identifies the external file to prevent the INPUT statement from moving to the next data line to complete reading information for an observation when the current data line is not as wide as expected.

Example Features

This example reads an external file that has the following features:

❑ Data values are aligned in columns.

❑ Records have variable lengths.

❑ No data values are missing.

The style of input used in this example is

❑ formatted input.

The INFILE statement options described in this example are the

❑ LRECL= option

❑ PAD option

❑ TRUNCOVER option.

External File

This external file contains four data lines that represent publisher information.

```
Media Source         New York
Tech Ref Publications  Massachusetts
Midwest Books Supply   Wisconsin
Business Resources     Utah
```

The two fields in each data line in order are:

1. name of the publisher

2. state of the publisher.

The data values are column aligned. The width of the data lines is variable.

Resulting Data Set

Output 2.11a PROC PRINT of PUBLISHERS Data Set

```
                               Publishers

      Obs      publishername              publisherstate


       1       Media Source               New York
       2       Tech Ref Publications      Massachusetts
       3       Midwest Books Supply       Wisconsin
       4       Business Resources         Utah
```

Program

This DATA step reads an external file where the data lines in the external file are variable in length and the data values are aligned in columns.

```
data publishers;
   infile 'c:\readdata\example2_11.dat'
           truncover;
```

Prevent the INPUT statement from moving to the next data line if the current data line is not as wide as the INPUT statement expects.

Read the data with formatted input. Define informats for the two variables so that they have a length long enough to hold the data values. Assign a length of 25 bytes to the variable PUBLISHERNAME.

```
   input @1  publishername $25.
```

Assign a length of 15 bytes to the variable PUBLISHERSTATE.

```
         @27 publisherstate $15.;
run;
proc print data=publishers;
   title 'Publishers';
run;
```

A Closer Look

Comparing FLOWOVER, MISSOVER, STOPOVER, and TRUNCOVER

Four INFILE statement options control reading of variable length data lines:

- FLOWOVER (the default)
- MISSOVER
- STOPOVER
- TRUNCOVER.

In most cases, **either FLOWOVER or TRUNCOVER option is desired.**

The **FLOWOVER** option causes the INPUT statement to continue to read the next data line if it does not find enough data in the current data line for all the variables specified by the INPUT statement. This is the default action of the INFILE statement. If the INPUT statement moves to the next input data line because it did not find values in the current data line, SAS writes the following message to the SAS log:

```
NOTE: SAS went to a new line when INPUT statement
reached past  the end of a line.
```

The **MISSOVER** option prevents the INPUT statement from reading a new data line when it does not find values in the current input data line for all the variables in the statement. With MISSOVER in effect, when the INPUT statement reaches the end of the data line, SAS sets all remaining variables without values to missing. If a variable's value at the end of the data line is not as wide as expected, SAS sets that variable's value to missing.

The MISSOVER and TRUNCOVER options both prevent the INPUT statement from reading a new data line when it does not find values in the current input data line. The difference between the two is that TRUNCOVER assigns what is available in the data line to variables. If the width of the last variable is less than expected, TRUNCOVER assigns what is there to the variable. The MISSOVER option sets the value of that variable to missing instead.

The **STOPOVER** option stops a DATA step when the INPUT statement reaches the end of the current data line and does not find values for all the variables specified on the statement.

The **TRUNCOVER** option, as shown in this example, prevents the INPUT statement from reading a new data line when it does not find values in the current data line for all variables in the statement. With TRUNCOVER in effect, when the INPUT statement reaches the end of the data line, SAS reads what is available, even if the width of the value is less than expected. SAS sets all remaining variables without values to missing.

Removing the TRUNCOVER Option from the Example

If you remove the TRUNCOVER option from the INFILE statement, SAS writes only two observations to the PUBLISHERS data set since the data lines are variable in length.

```
infile 'c:\readdata\example2_11.dat';
```

When reading PUBLISHERSTATE from the first data line, the INPUT statement does not find 15 columns of information so it moves to the next input data line to read PUBLISHERSTATE. It assigns the value **Tech Ref Public** to PUBLISHERSTATE.

In the second iteration of the DATA step, the INPUT statement starts reading the external file at the third data line. The value for PUBLISHER is **Midwest Books Supply**. Again, the INPUT statement does not find 15 columns of information in the current data line for PUBLISHERSTATE so it moves to the fourth data line to read PUBLISHERSTATE. The value of PUBLISHERSTATE becomes **Business Resour**. A PROC PRINT of the data set that results follows.

Output 2.11b PROC PRINT of
PUBLISHERS Data Set

```
                                   Publishers                                    1

           Obs      publishername              publisherstate

            1       Media Source               Tech Ref Public
            2       Midwest Books Supply        Business Resour
```

If the four data lines of this external file are fixed in length (each data line's length is 41 bytes), you would not need to specify the TRUNCOVER option. In that situation, SAS would create four observations from the four data lines.

Comparing the TRUNCOVER and PAD Options When Reading Variable Length Data

The PAD option in conjunction with the MISSOVER option on the INFILE statement behave similarly to the TRUNCOVER option. The MISSOVER and TRUNCOVER options each prevent SAS from moving to the next data line when the current data line is not as wide as coded for on the INPUT statement.

The TRUNCOVER option causes SAS to read what is available in the data line, either to the end of the data line or to the length specified by the value of the LRECL= option, whichever comes first.

The PAD option pads input data lines with blanks from the last character in the data line to the length specified by the value of the LRECL= option. This causes SAS to read to the length specified by the value of the LRECL= option. Each data line now looks like a fixed length record to SAS.

When working with variable length data, it is more efficient to use the TRUNCOVER option than the PAD and MISSOVER options because SAS stops reading the data line when it runs out of data. With the PAD option, SAS adds the steps of adding blanks to the length specified by the LRECL= option and then reads to the end of the data line, even if no data values are present.

The LRECL= option always has a value. SAS sets a default value for this option that varies depending on your operating system. You can override this default with the value you require by assigning that value to the LRECL= option on the INFILE statement.

Example 2.12 Processing Missing and Incomplete Data When Reading Column Aligned Data from Variable Length Data Lines

Goal

Read an external file where the data lines are variable in length and only one data line should be read per observation. The data values are aligned in columns. Any variables whose values are missing or incomplete should be set to missing.

Strategy

Add the MISSOVER option to the INFILE statement that identifies the external file in order to prevent the INPUT statement from moving to the next data line when the current data line is not as wide as expected, and also to set to missing any variables without values or whose values are incomplete.

Example Features

This example reads an external file that has the following features:

❑ Data values are aligned in columns.

❑ Records have variable lengths.

❑ Some data values are missing.

❑ Some numeric data values are nonstandard.

The style of input used in this example is

❑ formatted input.

The INFILE statement option described in this example is the

❑ MISSOVER option.

External File

This external file contains six data lines. Each data line contains sales information for an employee for a specific date.

```
EMP0312   28SEP2003    2509.32 MMW
EMP0381   28SEP2003    2699.89 TXP
EMP0543   28SEP2003    9006.19
EMP0387   28SEP2003     875.39 T
EMP0432   28SEP2003
EMP0382   28SEP2003   19392.38 LII
```

The data values are aligned in columns and the layout follows.

Field	Column Range
Employee ID	1–7
Sales Date	10–18
Sales Amount	20–28
Supervisor Initials	30–33

The values for supervisor initials are missing in data lines 3 and 5. The value for supervisor initials in the fourth data line is incomplete since only one letter of the three expected is specified. The sales amount is also missing in data line 5.

Resulting Data Set

Output 2.12 PROC PRINT of SALES Data Set

```
                              Sales Data

              employee_
    Obs          id          salesdate    salesamount    supvinits


     1         EMP0312        28SEP2003     $2,509.32        MMW
     2         EMP0381        28SEP2003     $2,699.89        TXP
     3         EMP0543        28SEP2003     $9,006.19
     4         EMP0387        28SEP2003       $875.39
     5         EMP0432        28SEP2003
     6         EMP0382        28SEP2003    $19,392.38        LII
```

Program

This program reads an external file where the data lines in the external file are variable in length and the data values are aligned in columns.

```
data sales;
   infile 'c:\readdata\example2_12.dat'
          missover;
```

Prevent the INPUT statement from reading the next data line when the current data line is not as wide as expected. Set variables whose values are incomplete to missing.

Read the external file with formatted input.

```
   input @1  employee_id $7.
         @10 salesdate    date9.
         @20 salesamount  8.
         @30 supvinits    $3.;
   format salesdate date9. salesamount dollar12.2;
run;

proc print data=sales;
   title 'Sales Data';
run;
```

A Closer Look

Comparing the FLOWOVER, MISSOVER, STOPOVER, and TRUNCOVER Options

See the discussion in "A Closer Look" in Example 2.11 that compares the FLOWOVER, MISSOVER, STOPOVER, and TRUNCOVER options.

Example 2.13 Stopping a DATA Step If Data Values Are Not Found in the Current Data Line

Goal

Read an external file where the data lines are variable in length and only one data line should be read per observation. The data values are aligned in columns. Stop the DATA step if the INPUT statement does not find values for all the variables as specified by the INPUT statement.

Strategy

Add the STOPOVER option to the INFILE statement that identifies the external file. The STOPOVER option stops the DATA step if the INPUT statement does not find values in the current data line for all variables named in the INPUT statement. View the SAS log after the DATA step executes to see if SAS stopped the DATA step.

Example Features

This example reads an external file that has the following features:

❐ Data values are aligned in columns.

❐ Records have variable lengths.

❐ Some data values are missing.

❐ Some numeric data values are nonstandard.

The style of input used in this example is

❐ formatted input.

The INFILE statement option described in this example is the

❐ STOPOVER option.

External File

This external file contains six data lines. Each data line contains sales information for an employee for a specific date.

```
EMP0312   28SEP2003    2509.32   MMW
EMP0381   28SEP2003    2699.89   TXP
EMP0543   28SEP2003    9006.19
EMP0387   28SEP2003     875.39   T
EMP0432   28SEP2003
EMP0382   28SEP2003   19392.38   LII
```

The data values are aligned in columns and the layout follows.

Field	Column Range
Employee ID	1–7
Sales Date	10–18
Sales Amount	20–28
Supervisor Initials	30–33

The value for supervisor initials is missing in data lines 3 and 5. In data line 4, the value for supervisor initials is incomplete since only one letter of the three expected is specified. The sales amount is also missing in data line 5.

Resulting Data Set

Output 2.13 PROC PRINT of SALES Data Set

```
                              Sales Data

              employee_
       Obs       id        salesdate     salesamount     supvinits


        1      EMP0312      28SEP2003      $2,509.32         MMW
        2      EMP0381      28SEP2003      $2,699.89         TXP
```

Program

This DATA step reads an external file where the data lines in the external file are variable in length and the data values are aligned in columns.

```
data sales;
   infile 'c:\readdata\example2_12.dat'
        stopover;
```

🔍 **Stop the DATA step if SAS reaches the end of the data line and data values are incomplete or missing as specified in the INPUT statement.**

Read the data with formatted input.

```
   input @1  employee_id  $7.
         @10 salesdate     date9.
         @21 salesamount   8.
         @30 supvinits     3.;
   format salesdate date9. salesamount dollar12.2;
run;
proc print data=sales;
   title 'Sales Data';
run;
```

🔍 **A Closer Look**

Understanding the Actions of the STOPOVER Option on the INFILE Statement

The DATA step in this example stops when reading the third data line because this data line is not as wide as expected; the value for SUPVINITS is missing.

If the STOPOVER option was not specified, the INPUT statement would have gone to the fourth data line to read SUPVINITS. The value of SUPVINITS for the third observation in that situation would be **EMP**.

When SAS encounters a data line that is not as wide as expected and STOPOVER is specified, SAS sets the automatic variable _ERROR_ to 1. This error condition causes SAS to write messages to the SAS log about the suspected source of the error. The values of the variables in the program data vector when the error occurred are displayed as well.

The SAS log for the example follows. Note that the ERROR message identifies that the INPUT statement exceeded the actual record length of the third data line.

```
426   data sales;
427      infile 'c:\readdata\example2_12.dat' stopover ;
428
429      input @1   employee_id $7.
430            @10 salesdate    date9.
431            @20 salesamount 8.
432            @30 supvinits    $3.;
433
434      format salesdate date9. salesamount dollar12.2;
435   run;
NOTE: The infile 'c:\readdata\example2_12.dat' is:
      File Name=c:\readdata\example2_12.dat,
      RECFM=V,LRECL=256

ERROR: INPUT statement exceeded record length.
       INFILE c:\readdata\example2_12.dat OPTION
       STOPOVER specified.
RULE:      ----+----1----+----2----+----3----+----4----
3          EMP0543   28SEP2001   9006.19
employee_id=EMP0543 salesdate=28SEP2001
salesamount=$9,006.19 supvinits=  _ERROR_=1 _N_=3
NOTE: 3 records were read from the infile
      'c:\readdata\example2_12.dat'.
      The minimum record length was 28.
      The maximum record length was 32.
NOTE: The SAS System stopped processing this step
      because of errors.
WARNING: The data set WORK.SALES may be incomplete.
When this step was stopped there were 2 observations
and 4 variables.
NOTE: DATA statement used:
      real time              0.06 seconds
```

Comparing FLOWOVER, MISSOVER, STOPOVER, and TRUN-COVER

See the discussion in "A Closer Look" in Example 2.11 that compares the FLOWOVER, MISSOVER, STOPOVER, and TRUNCOVER options.

CHAPTER 3
CONTROLLING HOW SAS READS EXTERNAL FILES

Introduction

After defining the structure of your external file to SAS through the use of the INFILE and FILENAME statements described in Chapter 2, you may need to add features to control how SAS reads your file. This chapter presents examples of using SAS language statements to control how SAS reads an external file.

Processes that you can control with options and statements for which there are examples in this chapter include

❏ reading only one data line per observation

❏ reading multiple data lines per observation

❏ reading multiple observations per data line

❏ examining the input data line so that a specific INPUT statement executes.

Example Overview

These tables present overviews of the features of the examples in this chapter.

Relationship Between Data Lines and Observations in Output Data Set	3.1	3.2	3.3	3.4	3.5	3.6	3.7	3.8	3.9	3.10	3.11	3.12	3.13	3.14
One data line defines one observation								●	●			●		●
Multiple data lines define one observation	●				●	●	●				●			
One data line defines multiple observations		●	●	●									●	
One data line modifies one observation											●			
INPUT Statement Features	3.1	3.2	3.3	3.4	3.5	3.6	3.7	3.8	3.9	3.10	3.11	3.12	3.13	3.14
Control which data line to read (# line pointer control)	●													
Control which data line to read (/ line pointer control)	●										●			
Reread a data line within an iteration of the DATA step (trailing at sign (@))			●	●		●	●		●	●			●	
Read multiple observations from one data line (double trailing at signs (@@))		●			●						●			
Read variable length variables ($VARYING informat)								●	●					
INFILE Statement Features	3.1	3.2	3.3	3.4	3.5	3.6	3.7	3.8	3.9	3.10	3.11	3.12	3.13	3.14
Define a variable that keeps track of the current location of the column pointer (COLUMN= option)			●											
Specify a character that delimits fields in an external file (DELIMITER= option)													●	
Create a variable that detects when SAS reads the last data line from an external file (END= option)						●	●							
Name a statement label that SAS directs processing to when it reaches the end of the external file (EOF= option)											●			
Define a variable that keeps track of the length of the current input line (LENGTH= option)			●						●					
Specify the length of the input record (LRECL= option)									●					
Prevent SAS from moving to a newinput line when the current input line is not as wide as expected (TRUNCOVER option)	●					●		●			●		●	●
Other Features	3.1	3.2	3.3	3.4	3.5	3.6	3.7	3.8	3.9	3.10	3.11	3.12	3.13	3.14
Using _INFILE_ automatic variable						●			●					
Using _IORC_ automatic variable													●	
Using _N_ automatic variable						●					●			
Using FIRSTOBS= and OBS= options											●			
Reading data with the INPUT function														●
Using the macro facility													●	
Some numeric data values are nonstandard														●
Specifying the MISSING statement												●		
Specifying the MODIFY statement													●	

Example 3.1 Reading Multiple Data Lines to Create a Single Observation

Goal

Read an external file where the data values for a single observation are on a known number of consecutive data lines.

Strategy

Read a specific number of data lines per iteration of the DATA step. This number corresponds to the number of data lines per observation.

Use the # line pointer control in the INPUT statement to designate the specific data line. Follow the # line pointer control with the names of the variables to be read from the data line. Include informats and other input instructions as required to read the variables.

Add TRUNCOVER to the INFILE statement to prevent SAS from moving to the next input line if the current line is not as wide as expected.

Example Features

The relationship between the data lines of the external file and the observations of the data set is that

❐ multiple data lines define one observation.

The INPUT statement features described in this example are

❐ # line pointer control

❐ / line pointer control.

The INFILE statement option used in this example is the

❐ TRUNCOVER option.

External File

The external file contains names and addresses.

```
Mary Patrick
313-555-9098
2440 West Maple Rd.
Trenton MI  48183
Gregory Higgins

1507 Knightdale Court
Harrisburg PA  19075
Don Lynx
608-555-1332
43 Madison East
Madison WI  54311
```

This external file contains the names, phone numbers, and addresses of three people. There are four data lines per person with one field per data line.

The fields in order are

1. name (data line 1)

2. phone number (data line 2)

3. address line 1 (data line 3)

4. address line 2 (data line 4).

The phone number for the second observation is missing (data line 6). A blank line serves as a placeholder for the phone number.

Resulting Data Set

Output 3.1 INFO Data Set

```
                    Address Information

Obs  name                phonenumber          address1


 1   Mary Patrick         3135559098   2440 West Maple Rd.
 2   Gregory Higgins               .   1507 Knightdale Court
 3   Don Lynx             6085551332   43 Madison East


Obs           address2
 1       Trenton MI 48183
 2       Harrisburg PA 19075
 3       Madison WI 54311
```

Program

The DATA step reads an external file where four consecutive data lines comprise the information for an observation.

```
data info;
   infile 'c:\readdata\example3_1.dat'
          truncover;
```

Prevent the INPUT statement from moving to the next data line if the current data line is not as wide as the INPUT statement expects.

Identify the specific data line in the set of four data lines per observation from which to read a variable. Read the data with formatted input.

```
   input #1 name $15.
         #2 phonenumber comma12.
         #3 address1 $30.
         #4 address2 $30.;
run;
```

```
proc print data=info;
   title 'Address Information';
run;
```

Related Technique

You can similarly read several data lines per observation by using the / line pointer control instead of the # line pointer control.

The # line pointer control is absolute and tells SAS the exact data line to read. By contrast, the / line pointer control is relative. SAS moves to the next data line when it encounters the / line pointer control in the INPUT statement.

When writing an INPUT statement with the / line pointer control, your code must account for all data lines per observation.

The DATA step that follows uses the / line pointer control. It creates the same data set as shown in Output 3.1.

```
data info;
   infile 'c:\readdata\example3_1.dat' truncover;
   input name $15. /
         phonenumber comma12. /
         address1 $30. /
         address2 $30.;
run;
```

A Closer Look

Reading Selected Data Lines with the # Line Pointer Control

You do not have to specify the variables for all the data lines that comprise an observation. You do need to indicate the total number of data lines per observation. To do this, specify a # line pointer control reference to the total number of data lines per observation.

The program that follows reads only the name and phone number from the external file for this example. The **#4** specifies that four data lines comprise the total number of data lines per observation.

```
data phoneinfo;
   infile 'c:\readdata\example3_1.dat'
         truncover;
   input #1 @1 name $15.
         #2 @1 phonenumber comma12.
         #4;
run;
```

Reading Selected Data Lines with the / Line Pointer Control

When using the / line pointer control, as with the # line pointer control, you do not have to specify the variables for all the data lines that comprise an observation. You must, however, include enough slashes to account for all the data lines that SAS should read per observation.

The program that follows reads only the name and phone number from the external file for this example. It uses the / line pointer control to indicate that there are four data lines per observation.

```
data phoneinfo;
   infile 'c:\readdata\example3_1.dat'
          truncover;
   input @1 name $15. /
         @1 phonenumber comma12.
         //;
run;
```

Example 3.2 Creating Multiple Observations from a Single Data Line

Goal

Read an external file where the information for multiple observations is in a single data line.

Strategy

Add the double trailing at signs (@@) to the INPUT statement to keep the data line in the input buffer across iterations of the DATA step. Write the INPUT statement to read the variables from one observation.

Example Features

The relationship between the data lines of the external file and the observations of the data set is that

❏ one data line defines multiple observations.

The INPUT statement feature described in this example is

❏ double trailing at signs (@@).

External File

The four data lines in this external file contain stock price information.

```
09/01/2003 . 09/02/2003 $45.00 09/03/2003 $46.38
09/04/2003 $42.33 09/05/2003 $38.88 09/08/2003 $37.73
09/09/2003 $40.87 09/10/2003 $40.55 09/11/2003 $35.33
09/12/2003 $32.01
```

Each data line contains data values for multiple observations. Two data values are recorded per observation—the date and stock price for that day. The three data lines contain information for ten observations.

The first stock price for the first day in the external file is missing. A period serves as a placeholder for the missing stock price.

Resulting Data Set

Output 3.2 STOCKPRICES Data Set

```
                Stock Price at End of Trading

        Obs       saledate       stockprice

         1       09/01/2003            .
         2       09/02/2003         $45.00
         3       09/03/2003         $46.38
         4       09/04/2003         $42.33
         5       09/05/2003         $38.88
         6       09/08/2003         $37.73
         7       09/09/2003         $40.87
         8       09/10/2003         $40.55
         9       09/11/2003         $35.33
        10       09/12/2003         $32.01
```

Program

Read the data with modified list input and formatted input. Specify the variables that should be read from one observation.

Place the double trailing @ (@@) at the end of the INPUT statement to hold a data line in the input buffer until SAS reads all observations from the data line. In this DATA step, SAS releases the data line when the pointer moves past the end of the input data line.

This DATA step reads multiple observations per data line.

```
data stockprices;
  infile 'c:\readdata\example3_2.dat';
  input saledate    mmddyy10.
        stockprice : comma8.2



        @@;

  format saledate mmddyy10. stockprice dollar8.2;
run;
proc print data=stockprices;
  title "Stock Price at End of Trading";
run;
```

A Closer Look

Reading Data for an Observation When Its Data Are on Consecutive Lines

The DATA step still executes correctly if the information for one observation is split over two data lines. By default, SAS moves to the next data line when it does not find all the information it expects on the current data line. This holds true even if the double trailing @ (@@) is in the INPUT statement.

In this example, that would mean for a given observation, the value for SALEDATE would be the last value on the data line and the value for STOCKPRICE would be the first value on the next data line.

Viewing the Message Generated by Using the Double Trailing @ (@@)

When you use the double trailing @ (@@), SAS always writes the following message to the SAS log.

NOTE: SAS went to a new line when INPUT statement
       reached past the end of a line.

Understanding the Double Trailing @ (@@) and the TRUNCOVER and MISSOVER Options

Do not specify the INFILE options TRUNCOVER or MISSOVER when using the double trailing @ (@@) in the INPUT statement. SAS will not execute a DATA step that has the MISSOVER option in the INFILE statement and the double trailing @ (@@) on the INPUT statement. A DATA step with the TRUNCOVER option in the INFILE statement and the double trailing @ (@@) in the INPUT statement executes indefinitely unless your DATA step contains logic to prevent this.

Example 3.3 Creating Multiple Observations from a Single Data Line and Retaining Identifier Information from the Data Line for Each Observation

Goal

Read an external file where the data values for a known number of observations are on a single data line. Include with each of the observations read from a data line the identifier information that is specified once at the beginning of that data line. Each data line contains the same known number of observations.

Strategy

Write two INPUT statements. Read the identifier information with the first INPUT statement. Add a trailing @ to this INPUT statement to hold the data line in the input buffer so that it can be read by the second INPUT statement.

Since a specific number of observations are known to be on each data line, write a DO loop that iterates that number of times. Place the second INPUT statement within the DO loop. Include a trailing @ at the end of this INPUT statement in order to keep the data line in the input buffer throughout execution of the DO loop.

Example Features

The relationship between the data lines of the external file and the observations of the data set is that

❐ one data line defines multiple observations.

The INPUT statement feature used in this example is a

❐ trailing @.

The INFILE statement options used in this example are the

❐ COLUMN= option

❐ LENGTH= option.

External File

This external file contains six data lines with temperature measurements recorded at three different locations at three different times on two days.

```
Lake 10/10/2001    8:00 38    16:00 47    24:00 42
City 10/10/2001    8:00 40    16:00 58    24:00 45
Yard 10/10/2001    8:00 33    16:00 52    24:00 41
Lake 10/17/2001    8:00 32    16:00 35    24:00 34
City 10/17/2001    8:00 32    16:00 40    24:00 37
Yard 10/17/2001    8:00 28    16:00 36    24:00 30
```

The data values are aligned in columns and the layout follows.

Field	Column Range
Location of Measurement	1–4
Date of Measurement	6–15
Time of Measurement 1	19–23
Temperature Measurement 1	25–26
Time of Measurement 2	30–34
Temperature Measurement 2	36–37
Time of Measurement 3	41–45
Temperature Measurement 3	47–48

The values for location and date of measurement on a data line should be retained with each of the three observations on the same data line.

Resulting Data Set

Output 3.3 OCTOBERTEMPS Data Set

```
                     Temperature Readings

   Obs    location    datemeasured    timemeasured     tempf

    1       Lake       10/10/2001        8:00  AM        38
    2       Lake       10/10/2001        4:00  PM        47
    3       Lake       10/10/2001       12:00  AM        42
    4       City       10/10/2001        8:00  AM        40
    5       City       10/10/2001        4:00  PM        58
    6       City       10/10/2001       12:00  AM        45
    7       Yard       10/10/2001        8:00  AM        33
    8       Yard       10/10/2001        4:00  PM        52
    9       Yard       10/10/2001       12:00  AM        41
   10       Lake       10/17/2001        8:00  AM        32
   11       Lake       10/17/2001        4:00  PM        35
   12       Lake       10/17/2001       12:00  AM        34
   13       City       10/17/2001        8:00  AM        32
   14       City       10/17/2001        4:00  PM        40
   15       City       10/17/2001       12:00  AM        37
   16       Yard       10/17/2001        8:00  AM        28
   17       Yard       10/17/2001        4:00  PM        36
   18       Yard       10/17/2001       12:00  AM        30
```

Program

This DATA step reads three observations per data line and retains information read at the beginning of the data line with each of the three observations.

```
data octobertemps;
   infile 'c:\readdata\example3_3.dat';
```

Read the identifier information for each group of three observations. Read the data with formatted input.

```
input @1 location $4. +1
          datemeasured mmddyy10.
```

Keep the current data line in the input buffer so that further processing can input the rest of the data line.

```
   @;
```

Drop the variable since it is not needed in the output data set.

```
drop i;
format datemeasured mmddyy10.
       timemeasured timeampm8.;
```

Read each of the three time and temperature measurements from the same data line.

```
do i=1 to 3;
```

Read each observation with formatted input.

```
   input +3 timemeasured time5.
         +1 tempf 2.
```

Keep the data line in the input buffer for the duration of the DO loop.

```
         @;
```

Write each measurement to the output data set.

```
   output;
end;
```

Do not include an INPUT; statement to release the data line from the input buffer. SAS automatically does this at the end of the iteration of the DATA step.

```
run;
proc print data=octobertemps;
   title "Temperature Readings";
run;
```

🔍 A Closer Look

Understanding the Processing of This DATA Step

This DATA step iterates seven times, once for each of the six data lines in the external file and a seventh time when it detects the end of the external file. On the seventh iteration, the DATA step stops after the INFILE statement executes and detects that there is no more input data.

The INPUT statement in the iterative DO loop executes three times for each of the first six iterations of the DATA step. The trailing @ in the INPUT statement in the DO loop keeps the data line in the input buffer so that three observations are read from one data line. The output data set, OCTOBERTEMPS, contains eighteen observations.

Since each of the first six iterations of the DATA step completely reads a data line, you do not need a RETAIN statement, but you do need an OUTPUT statement.

You do not need a RETAIN statement to save the values of the two fields at the beginning of a data line for inclusion with each of the three observations created from the data line. The values of LOCATION and DATEMEASURED remain available throughout one iteration of the DATA step.

This DATA step requires an OUTPUT statement to write each of the three observations to OCTOBERTEMPS. If you don't include an OUTPUT statement in a DATA step, SAS automatically creates output for you at the end of the iteration of the DATA step.

Without an OUTPUT statement, SAS would create only one observation from each data line. This observation would contain only data for the third measurement. Therefore, the OUTPUT statement is placed within the DO loop after data for an observation has been read so that output can be created with each iteration.

Related Technique

The above program requires three measurements per data line. The DATA step may execute with errors if there are less than three measurements per data line. If there are more than three measurements per data line, SAS ignores the data after the third measurement.

Statements can be added to the DATA step and options added to the INFILE statement so that the DATA step can read an undetermined number of observations per data line.

Options to consider including in the INFILE statement are COLUMN= and LENGTH=. The COLUMN= option names a variable that SAS sets to the current column location of the input pointer. The LENGTH= option names a variable that SAS sets to the length of the current input line.

A DO loop can test when the value of the COLUMN= variable exceeds the value of the LENGTH= variable. When this occurs, SAS has completely read the data line. A program that uses these two options follows. It produces the same data set as shown in Output 3.3.

Define a variable that SAS sets to the column location of the input pointer.

Define a variable that SAS sets to the length of the current input line.

Read time and temperature pairs until the value of POINTER is greater than DATALINELENGTH, which indicates that SAS has completely read the data line.

Read the data values with list input and group the variables and informats.

```
data octobertemps;
    infile 'c:\readdata\example3_3.dat'
            column=pointer


            length=datalinelength;

    input @1 location $4. +1 datemeasured mmddyy10. @;

    format datemeasured mmddyy10.
            timemeasured timeampm8.;
    do until (pointer gt datalinelength);




        input (timemeasured tempf) (+3 time5. +1 2.) @;
        output;
    end;
run;
```

Example 3.4 Reading Repeating Data Values When the Number of Repeating Data Values Is Known

Goal

Read a field in a data line that specifies the number of repeating data values to read from the rest of the data line. Create output for an observation for each set of repeating values in the data line. Retain constant information found on each data line with all the observations generated from the data line.

Strategy

Write an INPUT statement to read the constant information that should be retained for all observations generated from the data line. Also have this INPUT statement read the number of remaining fields in the data line. Keep this data line in the input buffer by adding a trailing at sign (@) to this statement.

Specify as the upper index of an iterative DO loop the variable that holds the number of remaining fields in the data line. Within the DO loop, write an INPUT statement to read the additional fields. Include a trailing @ in the INPUT statement to keep the data line in the input buffer for all iterations of the DO loop. Follow the INPUT statement with an OUTPUT statement to write out the observation derived from one iteration of the DO loop.

Example Features

The relationship between the data lines of the external file and the observations of the data set is that

❒ one data line defines multiple observations.

The INPUT statement feature used in this example is a

❒ trailing @.

External File

The external file holds grades for tests, quizzes, and homework for several students.

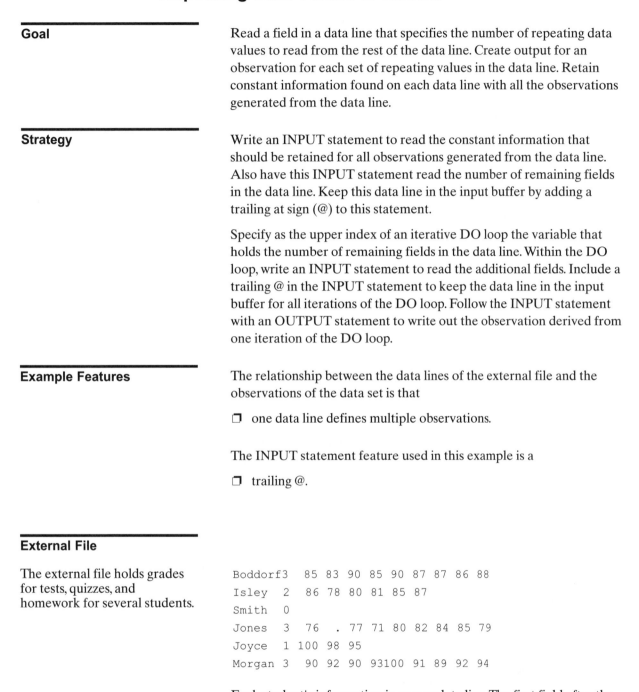

```
Boddorf3   85 83 90 85 90 87 87 86 88
Isley   2   86 78 80 81 85 87
Smith   0
Jones   3   76  . 77 71 80 82 84 85 79
Joyce   1 100 98 95
Morgan 3   90 92 90 93100 91 89 92 94
```

Each student's information is on one data line. The first field after the student's name is the number of time periods with grades. The remainder of the data line contains grades from each of the time periods. Three grades are recorded for each time period:

❒ test

❒ quiz

❒ homework.

Note that Smith has no grades for any time period and that Jones has no grade for the first quiz.

Each grade is three bytes wide.

Resulting Data Set

Output 3.4 GRADES Data Set

```
                    Grades for Several Periods


    Obs    lastname      period     test     quiz     homework


     1     Boddorf          1        85       83         90
     2     Boddorf          2        85       90         87
     3     Boddorf          3        87       86         88
     4     Isley            1        86       78         80
     5     Isley            2        81       85         87
     6     Jones            1        76        .         77
     7     Jones            2        71       80         82
     8     Jones            3        84       85         79
     9     Joyce            1       100       98         95
    10     Morgan           1        90       92         90
    11     Morgan           2        93      100         91
    12     Morgan           3        89       92         94
```

Program

This DATA step reads an external file where multiple observations can be generated from a data line. Information in the data line determines how many observations to generate from the data line.

```
data grades;
   infile 'c:\readdata\example3_4.dat';
   input lastname $7. nperiods 1. +1
```

Read the student name and the number of grading periods with formatted input.
Keep the current data line in the input buffer so that further processing can input the rest of the data line.

```
         @;
```

Drop this variable since it is only needed during execution of the DATA step.

```
   drop nperiods;
```

Execute this loop only if the student has at least one grading period.

```
   if nperiods gt 0 then do;
```

Set the upper index of the DO loop to the number of grading periods and execute the next INPUT statement that many times.

```
      do period=1 to nperiods;
```

Read the three grades for the grading period with formatted intput.

```
        input (test quiz homework) (3.)
```

Keep the current data line in the input buffer so that further processing can input the grades for all periods in the data line.

```
                @;
```

Output an observation for each student's grading period.

```
          output;
        end;
      end;
```

Write a message to the SAS log to indicate when a student does not have a grading period. Do not output the observation.

```
      else do;
        put '****No grading periods specified for '
            lastname;
      end;
    run;
    proc print data=grades;
      title 'Grades for Several Periods';
    run;
```

Example 3.5 Creating a Single Observation from an Unknown Number of Data Lines

Goal

Read an external file where the fields for an observation are on multiple data lines. The number of data lines per observation varies. The number of fields to read per observation is known.

Strategy

Define an array that contains the fields that are read per observation. Write an iterative DO loop that iterates the number of times equal to the number of fields to read per observation. Read one field per iteration of the DO loop.

Place an INPUT statement to read the elements of the array within the DO loop. Include the double trailing at signs (@@) in the INPUT statement to hold the data line in the input buffer across iterations of the DATA step so that a new observation can be started from a data line that also contains data for the previous observation.

Example Features

The relationship between the data lines of the external file and the observations of the data set is that

❑ multiple data lines define one observation.

The INPUT statement feature used in this example is

❑ double trailing @ (@@).

External File

The external file contains hourly temperature measurements for three days.

```
62 63 63 62 . . . 66 70 72

73 77 81 83 86 89 90 88 87 85
78 74 . . 68 66 65 65 63 63
66 69 72 74 79 83 87 90 92 91
91 90 87 85 80 78 76 75 66 66
65 63 62 60 61 64 70 73 76 82
88 89 92 93 92 91 88 84 82 81
78 79
```

There are ten measurements per data line and a total of 72 measurements. Periods serve as placeholders for missing temperature measurements.

The 24 measurements for the first day are on the first three data lines. The 24 measurements for the second day start with the fifth measurement on the third data line and end with the eighth value on the fifth data line. The remaining 24 measurements correspond to the third day's results.

Resulting Data Set

Output 3.5 THREEDAYS DATA Set

```
                  Temperatures for Three Days

    Obs   daycount   temp1  temp2  temp3  temp4  temp5  temp6  temp7  temp8

     1       1        62     63     63     62     .      .      .      66
     2       2        68     66     65     65     63     63     66     69
     3       3        66     66     65     63     62     60     61     64


    Obs   temp9  temp10  temp11  temp12  temp13  temp14  temp15  temp16

     1     70      72      73      77      81      83      86      89
     2     72      74      79      83      87      90      92      91
     3     70      73      76      82      88      89      92      93


    Obs   temp17  temp18  temp19  temp20  temp21  temp22  temp23  temp24

     1     90      88      87      85      78      74      .       .
     2     91      90      87      85      80      78      76      75
     3     92      91      88      84      82      81      78      79
```

Program

This DATA step reads a varying number of data lines per observation from an external file. It reads 24 variables per observation.

```
data threedays;
   infile 'c:\readdata\example3_5.dat';
```

Define an array that contains the number of variables to read per observation.

```
   array temperature{24} temp1-temp24;
```

Drop this variable since it is only needed during execution of the DATA step.

```
   drop i;
```

Keep track of the number of days of measurements in the external file in the accumulator variable DAYCOUNT.

```
   daycount + 1;
```

Iterate a DO loop the number of times equal to the number of temperature variables per observation.

```
   do i=1 to 24;
```

Read the data with list input.

```
    input temperature{i}
```

Keep the data line in the input buffer across iterations of the DATA step so that SAS can start a new observation from a data line that also contains data for the previous observation.

```
            @@;
      end;
    run;
```

🔍 **A Closer Look**

Understanding the Processing of this DATA Step

By default, SAS outputs an observation at the bottom of a DATA step, at the end of the iteration of a DATA step. The DO loop in this DATA step reads 24 temperature measurements per iteration of the DATA step. After the DO loop executes at the bottom of this DATA step, SAS writes an observation to THREEDAYS.

This DATA step relies on the default action of the INFILE statement that causes an INPUT statement to continue to read the next input data line if it does not find values in the current data line for all the variables in the statement. The double trailing @ (@@) tells SAS to hold a data line in the input buffer across iterations of the DATA step since some data lines contain data for separate observations.

Example 3.6 Reading Data with Varying Record Layouts

Goal

Read an external file where the information for one observation is on several consecutive data lines. The first data line in the set of data lines for an observation always has the same record layout. The number of remaining data lines for an observation after the first varies. These remaining data lines have different layouts and can be in any order. A field in each data line determines the record's type and thus the remaining information found on the data line.

Strategy

Determine all the possible record types that you expect to find in the external file. Determine which of these record types signals the first data line in a series of consecutive data lines for an observation.

Write an INPUT statement to read only the data line's record type. Add the trailing at sign (@) to the INPUT statement to hold the data line in the input buffer so that further processing can determine how to input the rest of the data line.

Write a SELECT block that tests the record type. Write WHEN clauses based on the possible values of record type. For each record type, write an INPUT statement specific to the record type.

It can take several iterations of the DATA step to read all the data lines for an observation. Specify a RETAIN statement to retain across iterations of the DATA step the values of all variables read for an observation.

Include an OUTPUT statement to direct that output be created after all data lines for the observation are read. Determine when all data lines for an observation have been read by writing an IF-THEN-DO block to test the record type. When a record type for the first in the series of data lines has been detected, create output with the information retained for the previous observation before beginning to read information for the current observation. Before creating output from an observation, check to see if the current data line is the first in the external file. If it is, do not create output since no additional data has been read at that point.

After creating output from the observation, initialize to missing the variables whose values must be retained across iterations of the DATA step. (These are variables specified in the RETAIN statement.)

Add the END= option to the first INFILE statement to define a variable that SAS sets to **1** when it reaches the end of the external file. Add an IF-THEN statement at the end of the step to test the value of the END= variable. When its value is **1**, indicating SAS has read the last data line in the external file, execute an OUTPUT statement to write out this last observation to the data set.

Example Features

The relationship between the data lines of the external file and the observations of the data set is that

❏ multiple data lines define one observation.

The INPUT statement feature used in this example is the

❏ trailing @.

The INFILE statement options used in this example are

❏ END= option

❏ TRUNCOVER option.

External File

This file contains client information. The information for a client starts with the client's name on a data line. A variey of different records can follow for each client.

```
NWilliam E. Ghoat
EWilliam.Ghoat@itsuperstars.com
NChris Gomez
AOverland Park          KS 59381
P913-555-3434x9863
Ecb001@kansas.com
F913-555-4439
NLouis Taylor
NSusann Rose
ARiverside              CA 91999
CNo Commission on Last Sale
P714-555-3391
O$335876.76
NMegumi Nakagawa
ALihui                  HI 99889
P808/555-7876
CRequest for Catalog
```

Each data line has a record type in the first byte that determines the information found on the rest of the line.

The following table lists the record types and the fields found in each record type.

Note that the third client, Louis Taylor, has only one data line, an "N" type record.

Record Type	Fields (listed in the order found in the record)
A	Client's city, state, and zip code
C	Comment about the client
E	Client's email address
F	Client's fax phone number
N	Client's name
O	Client's order amount
P	Client's phone number

Note that the fourth client, Susann Rose, has an O-type data line. Assume that O-type records were not expected in this external file and thus an INPUT statement for O-type records is not coded.

Resulting Data Set

Output 3.6 ACCOUNTS DATA Set

```
                    Accounts Information

 Obs      name             city            state        zip

  1  William E. Ghoat                                     .
  2  Chris Gomez        Overland Park    KS             59381
  3  Louis Taylor                                         .
  4  Susann Rose        Riverside        CA             91999
  5  Megumi Nakagawa    Lihui            HI             99889


 Obs           comment              email

  1                          William.Ghoat@itsuperstars.com
  2                          cb001@kansas.com
  3
  4   No Commission on Last Sale
  5   Request for Catalog


 Obs       fax               phone

  1
  2   913-555-4439       913-555-3434x9863
  3
  4                      714-555-3391
  5                      808/555-7876
```

Program

This DATA step reads an external file where the number of data lines per observation can vary. The record layouts and the order of the data lines also vary.

```
data accounts;
  infile 'c:\readdata\example3_6.dat'
       truncover
```

Prevent the INPUT statement from moving to the next data line if the current data line is not as wide as the INPUT statement expects.

Define a variable that SAS sets to 1 when it reads the last data line in the external file.

```
       end=done;
```

Retain the values of specific variables across iterations of the DATA step.	`retain name city state zip comment email fax phone;`
Define the lengths of specific variables.	`length name $ 25 city $ 24 state $ 2` `       comment email $ 50 fax phone $ 20;`
Drop this variable since it is only needed during execution of the DATA step.	`drop rectype;`
Read the record type of the current data line.	`input rectype $1.`
Keep the current data line in the input buffer so that further processing can determine how to read the rest of the data line.	`    @;`
Check the value of RECTYPE. Execute the block when the current data line's record type is N and the data line is not the first in the external file.	`if rectype='N' and _n_ ne 1 then do;`
Write the previous observation to the data set.	`  output;`

Begin a new observation by initializing all the variables in the output data set to missing.	`  name=' ';`
	`  city=' ';`
	`  state=' ';`
	`  zip=.;`
	`  comment=' ';`
	`  email=' ';`
	`  fax=' ';`
	`  phone=' ';`
	`end;`

Write a SELECT block that tests the value of RECTYPE.	`select (rectype);`

Execute an INPUT statement based on the current data line's record type. Read the data with formatted input.	`  when ('A') input city $24. state $2. +1 zip 5.;`
	`  when ('C') input comment  $50.;`
	`  when ('E') input email $50.;`
	`  when ('F') input fax    $20.;`
	`  when ('N') input name   $25.;`
	`  when ('P') input phone $20.;`

Execute the OTHERWISE block if the record type is not in the list above.	`  otherwise do;`

List information in the SAS log. Display the unknown record type.	`put 'Unknown Record Type: ' rectype`
Display the position of the data line in the external file, which is equal to the number of iterations of the DATA step and stored in the automatic variable _N_.	`'for data line: ' _n_ /`

Display the contents of the input buffer, which is stored in the _INFILE_ automatic variable.	`_infile_;`
	`end;`
	`end;`

Output the last observation's values after SAS reads the last data line from the external file.	`if done then output;`
	`run;`
	`proc print data=accounts;`
	`title 'Accounts Information';`
	`run;`

A Closer Look

Understanding How this DATA Step Executes

This section illustrates with the first client's data how this DATA step executes by presenting the contents of the input buffer and the program data vector.

The program data vector display shows the values of the user-defined variables and the automatic variable _N_. The value of the _INFILE_ automatic variable is the same as the contents of the input buffer. The automatic variable, _ERROR_, is omitted from the display.

Statement executed:

```
infile 'c:\readdata\example3_6.dat' truncover end=done;
```

Input Buffer:

Program Data Vector:

DONE	NAME	CITY	STATE	ZIP	COMMENT	EMAIL	FAX	PHONE	RECTYPE	_N_
0										1

Statement executed:

```
input rectype $1. @;
```

Determine the record type of the data line.

Input Buffer: `NWilliam E. Ghoat`

Program Data Vector:

DONE	NAME	C I T Y	S T A T E	Z I P	COMMENT	EMAIL	F A X	P H O N E	R E C T Y P E	_N_
0									N	1

Statement executed:

```
if rectype='N' and _n_ ne 1 then do
```

This statement is false. The block does not execute. No changes are made to the program data vector or to the input buffer.

Input Buffer: `NWilliam E. Ghoat`

Program Data Vector:

DONE	NAME	C I T Y	S T A T E	Z I P	COMMENT	EMAIL	F A X	P H O N E	R E C T Y P E	_N_
0									N	1

Statement executed:

```
select (rectype);
    when ('N') input name $25.;
```

The INPUT statement starts reading NAME from column 2 since the trailing @ in the first INPUT statement not only holds the data line in the input buffer, but it maintains the position of the column pointer. The input buffer is cleared after the INPUT statement executes.

Input Buffer: `NWilliam E. Ghoat`

Program Data Vector:

DONE	NAME	C I T Y	S T A T E	Z I P	COMMENT	EMAIL	F A X	P H O N E	R E C T Y P E	_N_
0	William E. Ghoat								N	1

Statement executed:

```
if done then output;
```

This statement is false and does not execute. This ends the second iteration of the DATA step.

Input Buffer:

Program Data Vector:

DONE	NAME	C I T Y	S T A T E	Z I P	COMMENT	EMAIL	F A X	P H O N E	R E C T Y P E	_N_
0	William E. Ghoat								N	1

Statement executed:

```
infile 'c:\readdata\example3_6' truncover end=done;
```

Input Buffer:

Program Data Vector:

DONE	NAME	C I T Y	S T A T E	Z I P	COMMENT	EMAIL	F A X	P H O N E	R E C T Y P E	_N_
0	William E. Ghoat									2

Statement executed:

```
input rectype $1. $;
```

Determine the record type of the data line.

Input Buffer: `Ewilliam.Ghoat@itsuperstars.com`

Program Data Vector:

DONE	NAME	C I T Y	S T A T E	Z I P	COMMENT	EMAIL	F A X	P H O N E	R E C T Y P E	_N_
0	William E. Ghoat								E	2

Statement executed:

```
if rectype='N' and _n_ ne 1 then do;
```

This statement is false. The block does not execute. No changes are made to the program data vector or to the input buffer.

Input Buffer: `EWilliam.Ghoat@itsuperstars.com`

Program Data Vector:

DONE	NAME	C I T Y	S T A T E	Z I P	COMMENT	EMAIL	F A X	P H O N E	R E C T Y P E	_N_
0	William E. Ghoat								E	2

Statement executed:

```
select (rectype);
   when ('E') input email $50.;
```

The INPUT statement starts reading EMAIL from column 2. The input buffer is cleared after the INPUT statement executes.

Input Buffer: `EWilliam.Ghoat@itsuperstars.com`

Program Data Vector:

DONE	NAME	C I T Y	S T A T E	Z I P	COMMENT	EMAIL	F A X	P H O N E	R E C T Y P E	_N_
0	William E. Ghoat					William.Ghoat@itsuperstars.com			N	2

Statement executed:

```
if done then output;
```

This statement is false and does not execute. This ends the second iteration of the DATA step.

Input Buffer:

Program Data Vector:

DONE	NAME	C I T Y	S T A T E	Z I P	COMMENT	EMAIL	F A X	P H O N E	R E C T Y P E	_N_
0	William E. Ghoat					William.Ghoat@itsuperstars.com			N	2

Statement executed:

```
infile 'c:\readdata\example3_6.dat' truncover end=done;
```

Input Buffer:

Program Data Vector:

DONE	NAME	C I T Y	S T A T E	Z I P	COMMENT	EMAIL	F A X	P H O N E	R E C T Y P E	_N_
0	William E. Ghoat					William.Ghoat@itsuperstars.com				3

Statement executed:

```
input rectype $1. @;
```

Determine the record type of the data line.

Input Buffer: NChris Gomez

Program Data Vector:

DONE	NAME	C I T Y	S T A T E	Z I P	COMMENT	EMAIL	F A X	P H O N E	R E C T Y P E	_N_
0	William E. Ghoat					William.Ghoat@itsuperstars.com			N	3

Statement executed:

```
if rectype='N' and _n_ ne 1 then do;
   output;
```

The IF statement is true. The block executes and the OUTPUT statement writes the values of the variables NAME, CITY, STATE, ZIP, COMMENT, EMAIL, FAX, and PHONE to the data set. The DROP statement omits RECTYPE from the output data set. SAS does not write automatic variables to an output data set. The variable DONE specified with the END= option is considered an automatic variable and SAS does not write it to the data set.

Input Buffer: NChris Gomez

Program Data Vector:

DONE	NAME	C I T Y	S T A T E	Z I P	COMMENT	EMAIL	F A X	P H O N E	R E C T Y P E	_N_
0	William E. Ghoat					William.Ghoat@itsuperstars.com			N	3

Statements executed:

```
name=' ';
city=' ';
state=' ';
zip=.;
comment=' ';
email=' ';
fax=' ';
phone=' ';
```

The statements initialize the variables to missing for the second observation.

Input Buffer: `NChris Gomez`

Program Data Vector:

DONE	NAME	C I T Y	S T A T E	Z I P	COMMENT	EMAIL	F A X	P H O N E	R E C T Y P E	_N_
0									N	3

Examining the SAS Log for Messages About this DATA Step

The SELECT block contains an OTHERWISE block that executes when the value of RECTYPE is not found in the list above. In this example, one data line has a RECTYPE value of O. This data line corresponds to an order amount for the fourth observation, client Susann Rose. Since no specification for this type of data line was included in the SELECT block, no information from this data line is recorded in the output data set.

The OTHERWISE block writes the following messages to the SAS log when it processes this unknown record type.

```
Unknown Record Type: O for data line: 13
O$335876.76
```

Where to Go From Here

See Example 3.11 for more information on working with the automatic variable _N_.

Example 3.7   Reading Hierarchical Data Lines

Goal

Read an external file where the data lines are in hierarchical order with the highest level first. A field in each data line determines the level of the data line. There are a varying number of data lines per observation.

Strategy

Examine the hierarchical structure of the data. Determine what constitutes an observation. Use this information to determine the variables per observation and when to output an observation.

Start the DATA step by reading the data type of a data line. Keep the data line in the input buffer by adding a trailing at sign (@) to this first INPUT statement. Write a SELECT block with the record type as the select expression. Within the SELECT block, write an INPUT statement for each record type found in the external file.

Specify in a RETAIN statement the variables whose values should be held across iterations of the DATA step.

Define a variable that signals when specific levels of the hierarchy have been read. Use this variable as a true/false (1/0) variable to determine when to output an observation.

When the beginning of a new observation has been detected, write out the data for the previous observation and initialize the variables for this new observation to missing.

Add the END= option to the INFILE statement. At the end of the DATA step, test the value of the END= variable to determine if SAS has read the last data line in the external file. When it has read the last data line, create output for this last observation.

Example Features

The relationship between the data lines of the external file and the observations of the data set is that

❑ multiple data lines define one observation.

The INPUT statement feature used in this example is a

❑ trailing @.

The INFILE statement option used in this example is the

❑ END= option.

External File

This file contains information about teachers, students, and the classes the students are taking.

```
T Mary Smith              334
S Emily Livingston         15   333 East Shore Drive   Shoreview
C Algebra                   1
C History                   2
C Chemistry                 4
C Music                     5
S Jeremy Anderson          14   153 Winding Way        Shoreview
C Physics                   1
C English                   2
C Keyboarding               3
C Snowboarding              6
T John Schultz            331
S Katie Carlson            14   9873 South Blvd        Roseville
C Art History               1
C American Literature       2
S Sue Lee                  15   873 Valley Pkwy        Roseville
C Calculus                  1
C Creative Writing          2
C Computer Programming      3
S Rick Ramirez             15   65 Maple St.           Pleasant Lake
C Computer Programming      2
C Physical Education        3
```

The three types of records are arranged in a hierarchy. The number of students per teacher can vary with a minimum of one. The number of classes per student can vary with a minimum of one and a maximum of four.

The first field in each data line determines the type of the record. The data values are aligned in columns. The layout for the remaining fields and their positions in the hierarchy follow.

Hierarchy Level	Record Type	Field	Column Range
Top	T(Teacher)	Teacher Name	3–22
Top	T(Teacher)	Teacher Room Number	25–27
Middle	S(Student)	Student Name	3–22
Middle	S(Student)	Student Age	25–26
Middle	S(Student)	Student Home Address	30–52
Middle	S(Student)	Student Home City	54–66
Bottom	C(Class)	Class Name	3–22
Bottom	C(Class)	Class Period	24

Resulting Data Set

Output 3.7 STUDENTS Data Set

```
                 Student Information by Teacher

----------   teachername=John Schultz teacherroom=331 ----------

Obs     studentname      studentage     studentaddress      studentcity

1       Katie Carlson       14          9873 South Blvd    Roseville
2       Sue Lee             15          873 Valley Pkwy    Roseville
3       Rick Ramirez        15          65 Maple St.       Pleasant Lake


Obs    classname1                      classname2

1      Art History                 American Literature
2      Calculus                    Creative Writing
3      Computer Programming        Physical Education


Obs        classname3          classname4      classperiod1

1                                                   1
2          Computer Programming                     1
3                                                   2


Obs    classperiod2    classperiod3    classperiod4

1           2                .               .
2           2                3               .
3           3                .               .
------------ teachername=Mary Smith teacherroom=334 -----------

Obs    studentname        studentage    studentaddress          studentcity

4      Emily Livingston      15      333 East Shore Drive     Shoreview
5      Jeremy Anderson       14      153 Winding Way          Shoreview


Obs   classname1  classname2  classname3  classname4  classperiod1

4     Algebra     History     Chemistry   Music          1
5     Physics     English     Keyboarding Snowboarding    1


Obs classperiod2    classperiod3    classperiod4
4       2               4               5
5       2               3               6
```

Program

This DATA step reads an external file where the data lines are arranged hierarchically.

The output SAS data set contains one observation for each student, which is the record in the middle of the hierarchy.

```
data students;
   infile 'c:\readdata\example3_7.dat'
```

Define a variable that SAS sets to 1 when it reads the last data line in the external file.

```
              end=last;
```

Retain specific variables across iterations of the DATA step.

```
retain flag 0 teachername teacherroom
     studentname studentage studentaddress studentcity
     classname1-classname4 classperiod1-classperiod4;
```

Define the CLASSNAME and CLASSPERIOD arrays to have four elements, the maximum number of classes per student.

```
array classname{4}  $ 20 classname1-classname4;
array classperiod{4} classperiod1-classperiod4;
```

Drop these variables since they are only needed during execution of the DATA step.

```
drop classnum i flag type;
```

Read the record type and hold the data line in the input buffer.

```
input @1 type $1. @;
```

Write a SELECT block to evaluate TYPE.

```
select (type);
  when ('T') do;
```

Control when to write an observation to the STUDENTS data set by testing the value of FLAG. Write out the observation for the last student in the group of students assigned to a teacher with this IF statement.

```
    if flag then output;
```

Reset FLAG to zero to signal the beginning of a new student observation as well as a new teacher observation.

```
    flag=0;
```

Read the teacher data line with column input.

```
    input teachername $ 3-22 teacherroom 25-27;
  end;
  when ('S') do;
```

Start reading information about a student in this block. Check the value of FLAG to determine if data for a previous student has been retained. If so, write out the data retained for the previous student.

```
        if flag then output;
```

Reset the CLASSNUM counter that tallies the number of classes per student.

```
        classnum=0;
```

Reset FLAG to 0 to indicate that no class data has yet been read for this student.

```
        flag=0;
```

Initialize these variables to missing since this is the beginning of the information for a student.

```
        do i=1 to 4;
           classname{i}=' ';
           classperiod{i}=.;
        end;
```

Read the student data line with column input and modified list input.

```
        input studentname $ 3-22 studentage 25-26
              studentaddress $ 30-52 studentcity : $13.;
      end;
      when ('C') do;
```

Tally the number of classes per student. Use CLASSNUM later as the index variable that points to the fields in the arrays.

```
        classnum+1;
```

Set FLAG to 1 to indicate that the student has a class record.

```
        flag=1;
```

Read the class data line with column input.

```
        input classname{classnum} $ 3-22
              classperiod{classnum} 24;
      end;
      otherwise do;
        file log;
```

Execute this block if SAS detects an unknown record type. Write a message and the contents of the input buffer to the SAS log.

Display the data line with the unknown record type by writing out the value of the automatic variable, _INFILE_, which represents the contents of the input buffer.

```
        put 'Unknown Record Type: ' _infile_;
        delete;
      end;
   end;
```

Check if SAS has read the last data line in the external file. If so, write out the data for this student.

```
   if last then output;
run;
proc sort data=students;
   by teachername teacherroom;
run;
```

```
proc print data=students;
   title 'Student Information by Teacher';
   by teachername teacherroom;
run;
```

A Closer Look

Understanding When This DATA Step Outputs an Observation

This DATA step uses the FLAG variable to determine when to write output for an observation to the data set. Information about a student comprises an observation. A student is in the middle of the hierarchy between the teacher and the classes.

The DATA step writes out an observation when it completes reading all the courses for a student.

It detects that all courses have been read for a student by encountering a record higher in the hierarchy or by reaching the end of the external file. When the DATA step reads a teacher record or a different student's record, it determines that the previous student's information is complete.

For example, when Jeremy Anderson's S-type data line is put in the input buffer by reading TYPE, it causes SAS to write Emily Livingston's observation to the data set. Then SAS reads Jeremy's information. When John Schultz's T-type data line is put in the input buffer by reading TYPE, it causes Jeremy's observation to be output with the correct teacher name—Mary Smith—before the second teacher's (John Schultz) data are read.

Example 3.8   Reading Variable Width Data Values That Are Not Delimited

Goal

Read an external file where the width of a character data value varies from data line to data line. The width of the character data value is known, is specified as a field on the data line, and precedes the data value.

Strategy

Write an INPUT statement that reads the width of the character variable. In the same INPUT statement, read the character variable with the $VARYING*w.* informat. Specify the maximum width of the character variable with the $VARYING*w.* informat. Follow the $VARYING*w.* informat with the name of the variable that holds the width of the character field.

Example Features

The relationship between the data lines of the external file and the observations of the data set is that

❑   One data line defines one observation.

The INPUT statement feature used in this example is

❑ $VARYING informat.

The INFILE statement option used in this example is the

❑   TRUNCOVER option.

External File

This external file contains book order information for several libraries.

```
14Highland Hills31Prairie Plants for the Backyard04/03/20023
18West Lake Regional24101 Ways to Retire Early05/02/20025
05Maple39Bed and Breakfasts in the Upper Midwest05/01/20021
24Metropolitan Main Branch25Mammals of the Northwoods01/15/20022
24Metropolitan Main Branch16Investing Basics01/30/200210
24Metropolitan Main Branch18Auto Repair-Safely02/18/20022
05Maple16Halloween Baking09/01/20021
18West Lake Regional26Taking Care of Your Health01/19/20022
```

Each data line contains the following fields in order:

1.   field length of library name

2.   library name

3.   field length of book title

4.   book title

5.   order date (mm/dd/yyyy)

6.   number of copies ordered.

Two fields vary in length—the library name and the title of the book. The length of each of these fields precedes each field.

Resulting Data Set

Output 3.8 BOOKORDER Data Set

```
                    Books Ordered by Library

------------ libraryname=Highland Hills --------------

Obs          booktitle              orderdate    ncopies

1   Prairie Plants for the Backyard  04/03/2002        3


----------------- libraryname=Maple ------------------

Obs booktitle                        orderdate ncopies

2    Bed and Breakfasts in the Upper Midwest 05/01/2002    1
3    Halloween Baking                     09/01/2002       1


-------- libraryname=Metropolitan Main Branch ---------

Obs     booktitle                   orderdate    ncopies

4     Mammals of the Northwoods     01/15/2002        2
5     Investing Basics              01/30/2002       10
6     Auto Repair-Safely            02/18/2002        2


----------- libraryname=West Lake Regional ------------

Obs          booktitle             orderdate    ncopies

7    101 Ways to Retire Early     05/02/2002         5
8    Taking Care of Your Health   01/19/2002         2
```

Program

This DATA step reads an external file where two character fields are variable in width and the width of each of these fields is part of the data line.

<table>
<tr>
<td>

Prevent the INPUT statement from moving to the next data line if the current data line is not as wide as the INPUT statement expects.

</td>
<td>

```
data bookorder;
   infile 'c:\readdata\example3_8.dat'
              truncover;
```

</td>
</tr>
<tr>
<td>

Drop these two variables that hold the width of the two varying width character fields since they are not needed after execution of the DATA step.

</td>
<td>

```
   drop liblength titlelength;
```

</td>
</tr>
<tr>
<td>

Read the length of the LIBRARYNAME data value.

</td>
<td>

```
   input liblength 2.
```

</td>
</tr>
<tr>
<td>

Set the maximum length of LIBRARYNAME to 50 bytes with the $VARYING*w*.informat. Read the number of bytes equal to the current value of LIBLENGTH to obtain the current value of LIBRARYNAME.

</td>
<td>

```
         libraryname $varying50. liblength
```

</td>
</tr>
<tr>
<td>

Read the length of the BOOKTITLE field and store that value in TITLELENGTH.

</td>
<td>

```
         titlelength 2.
```

</td>
</tr>
<tr>
<td>

Set the maximum length of BOOKTITLE to 50 bytes with the $VARYING*w*. informat. Read the number of bytes equal to TITLELENGTH for BOOKTITLE.

</td>
<td>

```
         booktitle $varying50. titlelength
```

</td>
</tr>
<tr>
<td>

Read the order date and number of copies with formatted input.

</td>
<td>

```
         orderdate mmddyy10. ncopies 2.;

   format orderdate mmddyy10.;
run;
proc sort data=bookorder;
   by libraryname;
run;
proc print data=bookorder;
   title 'Books Ordered by Library';
   by libraryname;
run;
```

</td>
</tr>
</table>

A Closer Look

Specifying the $VARYING*w.* Informat

The syntax of the $VARYING*w.* is

```
$VARYINGw. length-variable
```

The *w* is optional. When specified, it defines the length of the variable if you did not define the length of the variable elsewhere in the DATA step. When you do not specify *w* and you do not define the length of the variable elsewhere, SAS by default assigns 8 as the length.

The *length-variable* is a variable in the DATA step. In this application, the value of this variable is part of the data line. In other applications, you may have to calculate this value. Example 3.9 presents such a program. The *length-variable* cannot be specified as an array reference.

Example 3.9 Reading Varying Width Data Values That Are Not Delimited and Calculating the Width within the DATA Step

Goal

Read an external file that contains character data values that are variable in width. The data values are not delimited. Calculate the length of the character data values in the DATA step.

Strategy

Obtain the length of the input data line by specifying the LENGTH= option in the INFILE statement. Define a variable with the LENGTH= option to hold the record length of the current input line.

Read the entire data line into a variable by specifying the $VARYING*w*. informat with the record length as this variable's width. Follow the $VARYING*w*. informat with the name of the LENGTH= variable. Add a trailing at sign (@) to the INPUT statement to hold the data line in the input buffer so that it can be read by the next INPUT statement.

Examine the variable that contains the data line. With the INDEX function, determine the position where the field following the varying width field starts. Subtract one from this position to obtain the width of the varying width field. Read the varying width field with the $VARYING*w*. informat and read the remaining fields in the data line.

Example Features

The relationship between the data lines of the external file and the observations of the data set is that

❐ one data line defines one observation.

The INPUT statement features used in this example are:

❐ trailing @

❐ $VARYING*w*. informat.

The INFILE statement options used in this example are

❐ LENGTH= option

❐ LRECL= option.

Other features of this example include the

❐ _INFILE_ automatic variable.

External File

This external file contains comments about recent restaurant visits.

```
My pasta was cold.$25.2010/01/2001
Service slow, food great.$38.7310/02/2001
More selection on the children's menu!!!$45.1110/02/2001
More off-street parking.$18.3810/02/2001
$20.8710/02/2001
Too noisy. Food bland. Menu overpriced.$27.6610/03/2001
```

Each data line contains information about one customer's visit. The fields on each data line in order are

❑ comment

❑ the bill

❑ the date (mm/dd/yyyy).

The comment is variable in length. No delimiters separate the three fields, but the bill field always starts with a dollar sign ($).

Note that no comment was recorded on the fifth data line.

Resulting Data Set

Output 3.9 COMMENTS Data Set

```
                    Recent Restaurant Comments

    Obs      comment                                   visitdate    bill


     1       My pasta was cold.                        10/01/2001  $25.20
     2       Service slow, food great.                 10/02/2001  $38.73
     3       More selection on the children's menu!!!  10/02/2001  $45.11
     4       More off-street parking.                  10/02/2001  $18.38
     5       No comment recorded.                      10/02/2001  $20.87
     6       Too noisy. Food bland. Menu overpriced.   10/03/2001  $27.66
```

Program

This DATA step reads an external file where the data values are not delimited and the first field is variable in length. The length of the first field is determined by examining the data line.

Define a variable that SAS sets to the length of the current input line.

```
data comments;
  infile 'c:\readdata\example3_9.dat'
         length=recordlength;
```

Specify the length of FULLRECORD to be sufficient to hold the entire data line.

```
length fullrecord $ 100 comment $ 90;
```

Drop these variables since they are needed only during execution of the DATA step.

```
drop fullrecord commentlength;
format visitdate mmddyy10. bill dollar6.2;
```

Read the entire data line into the variable FULLRECORD. Specify the width of the current value of FULLRECORD by following the $VARYING*w*.informat with the LENGTH= variable.

```
input fullrecord $varying. recordlength
```

Keep the current data line in the input buffer so that further processing can input the rest of the data line.

```
      @;
```

Examine the variable that contains the current input line. Look for the dollar sign ($), which signals the beginning of the second field. Calculate the length of the COMMENT field as one less than the column where the dollar sign was found.

```
commentlength=index(fullrecord,'$')-1;
```

Read the varying width field COMMENT with the $VARYING*w*. informat. Read the number of bytes equal to COMMENTLENGTH into the COMMENT variable.

```
input @1 comment $varying. commentlength
```

Read the remaining two variables with formatted input.

```
          bill comma6.2
          visitdate mmddyy10.;
```

Assign text to the COMMENT variable when a comment has been omitted from the data line.

```
  if comment=' ' then comment='No comment recorded.';
run;
proc print data=comments;
  title 'Recent Restaurant Comments';
run;
```

🔍 A Closer Look

More Information on the $VARYINGw. Informat

See "A Closer Look" for Example 3.8 for more information on the $VARYINGw. informat.

Understanding the Timing of the LENGTH= Option in the INFILE Statement

SAS does not assign a value to the LENGTH= variable until an INPUT statement executes. When the first INPUT statement executes in this example, SAS sets the value of the LENGTH= variable to the length of the current input line.

The first INPUT statement also references the LENGTH= variable. SAS sets the length of the LENGTH= variable before it reads the variables specified in the INPUT statement. Because the value of the LENGTH= variable is known, SAS correctly reads FULLRECORD.

Retaining the Value Assigned to the LENGTH= Variable

The LENGTH= variable is an automatic variable and SAS does not retain the variable in the output data set. If you want to save the value of the LENGTH= variable, assign it to a SAS data set variable.

Related Technique

Note that the _INFILE_ variable is available starting in version 7.

A simpler way of creating the COMMENTS data set does not require rereading the data line. This DATA step uses the SUBSTR function to obtain the variable values.

Instead of reading the entire data line into a variable, the DATA step works directly with the data in the input buffer. The designation, _INFILE_, represents the contents of the input buffer.

This DATA step would not execute correctly if the length of a data line exceeded the default record length set in your SAS session. For Windows and UNIX, the default is 256 bytes. If your data lines could exceed the default, add the LRECL= option to the INFILE statement. Specify that option to be equal to the maximum record length in your external file.

The COMMENTS data set produced by the following DATA step is identical to the one shown in Output 3.9.

```
data comments;
   infile 'c:\readdata\example3_9.dat';

   length comment $ 90;
   drop commentlength;
   format visitdate mmddyy10. bill dollar6.2;
```

Move a complete data line into the input buffer with this INPUT statement. Do not read any variables.

```
   input;

   commentlength=index(_infile_,'$')-1;
```

Extract text from the value of
INFILE.

```
if commentlength > 0 then
   comment=substr(_infile_,1,commentlength);
bill=input(substr(_infile_,commentlength+1,6),comma6.2);
visitdate=input(substr(_infile_,commentlength+7),
                mmddyy10.);

if comment=' ' then comment='No comment recorded.';
run;
```

Example 3.10   Detecting When SAS Reaches the End of an External File

---

Goal

Detect when SAS reaches the end of the external file that it is reading. When detected, summarize information about the data read from the external file and write the summary to the SAS log.

Strategy

Add the EOF= option to the INFILE statement to define a statement label that SAS directs processing to when it reaches the end of the external file. Write the statements that SAS should execute when it detects the end of the external file. Precede the first statement in this group with the label specified by the EOF= option.

Precede the label with a RETURN statement to prevent execution of the statements that follow the label with each iteration of the DATA step.

Example Features

The relationship between the data lines of the external file and the observations of the data set is that

❑ one data line defines multiple observations.

The INPUT statement features used in this example is

❑ double trailing @ (@@).

The INFILE statement option used in this example is the

❑ EOF= option.

External File

This external file contains sales amounts for states.

```
NY 339.29 CT 887.87 RI 8763.00 CT 87.98
GA 102.87 FL 978.67 FL 876.33 NH 351.98
MA 2347.01 FL 55361.33 GA 553.01 NH 653.22
NY 120987.33 NJ 999.99 NY 331.30 GA 77789.23
GA 8730.12 GA 5430.90 GA 152.07 CT 109.98
```

Several observations are on one data line. Each observation contains two variables: state and sales amounts for the state.

Resulting SAS Log

Output 3.10 Log showing summary information

```
*-*-*-*-*-*-*-*-*-*-*-*-*-*-*-*-*-*-*-*-*-*-*-*-*-*-*-*-*-*-*-*-*-
Region        Total Sales      N Sales    Average Sale
Northeast     $135,858.95        11       $12350.81
Southeast     $149,974.53         9       $16663.84
*-*-*-*-*-*-*-*-*-*-*-*-*-*-*-*-*-*-*-*-*-*-*-*-*-*-*-*-*-*-*-*-*-
```

Program

This DATA step reads an external file. When it detects the end of the external file, it summarizes information about the file and writes the summary to the SAS log. It does not create a data set.

```
data _null_;
  infile 'c:\readdata\example3_10.dat'
        eof=summary;
```

Direct processing to the label SUMMARY when SAS reaches the end of the external file.

```
  length state $ 2;
```

Read the data with list input.

```
  input state $ sales
```

Keep the data line in the input buffer across iterations of the DATA step so that SAS reads all the observations on a data line.

```
    @@;
```

Test the value of STATE and tally the number of sales and total sales for each of the two regions, Northeast and Southeast.

```
  if state in ('CT' 'MA' 'NH' 'NY' 'NJ' 'RI') then do;
    nsalesne+1;
    sumne+sales;
  end;
  else if state in ('GA' 'FL') then do;
    nsalesse+1;
    sumse+sales;
  end;
```

Stop the iteration of the DATA step and return to the beginning of the DATA step.

```
  return;
```

Once reaching the end of file, execute the statements that summarize the external file.

```
summary:
  if nsalesne > 0 then avgne=sumne/nsalesne;
  if nsalesse > 0 then avgse=sumse/nsalesse;
  put 29*'*-' /
'Region      Total Sales    N Sales   Average Sale'/
    'Northeast' @12 sumne dollar15.2 @35 nsalesne 2.
    @43 avgne dollar9.2 /
    'Southeast' @12 sumse dollar15.2 @35 nsalesse 2.
    @43 avgse dollar9.2 /
    29*'*-' ;
run;
```

A Closer Look

Comparing the EOF= and END= INFILE Statement Options

The EOF= and END= INFILE statement options provide the capability to control processing within the DATA step.

The specification for the EOF= option is a statement label that acts as an implied GOTO statement. When the INPUT statement tries to read from the input file and there are no more data lines to read, SAS transfers processing to the first statement following the statement label.

The END= option defines an automatic variable whose value is initialized as **0** and remains **0** until SAS reads the last data line in the input file. When reading the last data line in the input file, SAS sets the value of the END= variable to **1**.

Understanding Why the END= Option Would Not Execute as Required in this Example

The difference between the EOF= and END= INFILE statements options is described above. The example above demonstrates the use of the EOF= option. It would not execute correctly if you revised the DATA step to use the END= option instead of the EOF= option because of the multiple observations found on the last data line.

The following DATA step demonstrates the use of the END= option in this DATA step and how it affects the results.

Define a variable that SAS sets to 1 when it reads the last data line in the external file.

```
data _null_;
   infile 'c:\readdata\example3_10.dat'
          end=lastline;
   length state $ 2;
   input state $ sales @@;

   if state in ('CT' 'MA' 'NH' 'NY' 'NJ' 'RI') then do;
      nsalesne+1;
      sumne+sales;
   end;
   else if state in ('GA' 'FL') then do;
      nsalesse+1;
      sumse+sales;
   end;

   if lastline then do;
      if nsalesne > 0 then avgne=sumne/nsalesne;
      if nsalesse > 0 then avgse=sumse/nsalesse;
      put 29*'*-' /
   'Region        Total Sales      N Sales    Average
Sale'/
         'Northeast' @12 sumne dollar15.2 @35 nsalesne 2.
         @43 avgne dollar9.2 /
         'Southeast' @12 sumse dollar15.2 @35 nsalesse 2.
         @43 avgse dollar9.2 /
         29*'*-' ;
   end;
run;
```

Test if SAS is processing the last data line in the external file. If so, execute the statements in this block.

The value of the variable LASTLINE is **1** for each of the four observations read from the last data line. The following SAS log shows that the statements in the DO block execute four times.

Resulting SAS Log

Output 3.10b Log showing summary information when using the END= option

```
*-*-*-*-*-*-*-*-*-*-*-*-*-*-*-*-*-*-*-*-*-*-*-*-*-*-*-*-*-*-*-
Region          Total Sales        N Sales     Average Sale
Northeast       $135,748.97          10        $13574.90
Southeast       $144,391.56           7        $20627.37
*-*-*-*-*-*-*-*-*-*-*-*-*-*-*-*-*-*-*-*-*-*-*-*-*-*-*-*-*-*-*-

*-*-*-*-*-*-*-*-*-*-*-*-*-*-*-*-*-*-*-*-*-*-*-*-*-*-*-*-*-*-*-
Region          Total Sales        N Sales     Average Sale
Northeast       $135,748.97          10        $13574.90
Southeast       $149,822.46           8        $18727.81
*-*-*-*-*-*-*-*-*-*-*-*-*-*-*-*-*-*-*-*-*-*-*-*-*-*-*-*-*-*-*-

*-*-*-*-*-*-*-*-*-*-*-*-*-*-*-*-*-*-*-*-*-*-*-*-*-*-*-*-*-*-*-
Region          Total Sales        N Sales     Average Sale
Northeast       $135,748.97          10        $13574.90
Southeast       $149,974.53           9        $16663.84
*-*-*-*-*-*-*-*-*-*-*-*-*-*-*-*-*-*-*-*-*-*-*-*-*-*-*-*-*-*-*-

*-*-*-*-*-*-*-*-*-*-*-*-*-*-*-*-*-*-*-*-*-*-*-*-*-*-*-*-*-*-*-
Region          Total Sales        N Sales     Average Sale
Northeast       $135,858.95          11        $12350.81
Southeast       $149,974.53           9        $16663.84
*-*-*-*-*-*-*-*-*-*-*-*-*-*-*-*-*-*-*-*-*-*-*-*-*-*-*-*-*-*-*-
```

You may be able to use the END= option with your application if your external file does not require the use of the double trailing @ (@@) to read multiple observations from the last data line.

Example 3.11 Limiting the Number of Data Lines Read from an External File

Goal

Read a specific number of data lines from an external file and start reading from a specific line of data within the external file.

Strategy

Specify the maximum number of data lines to read with the OBS= INFILE statement option. Specify the data line where the reading should begin with the FIRSTOBS= INFILE statement option.

Example Features

The relationship between the data lines of the external file and the observations of the data set is that

❑ multiple data lines define one observation.

The INFILE statement option used in this example is the

❑ TRUNCOVER option.

Other features of this example include

❑ FIRSTOBS= and OBS= options

❑ _N_ automatic variable.

External File

This external file contains the titles and publishing information for a book order.

```
Everyday Web Page Construction
2002 IT Publishing                San Francisco
Strategic Data Mining
2002 Smith, Anderson, Carlson    New York
Retirement Planning for the Next Generation
2002 Home Publishers             Chicago
How to Cope with Busy Teenage Schedules
2002 Home Publishers             Chicago
Favorite Dogs Calendar 2003
2002 Home Publishers             Chicago
Reading Spreadsheet Data
2002 Smith, Anderson, Carlson    New York
```

The information for one observation takes two consecutive data lines with the book title on the first and the publishing information on the second.

The data values are aligned in columns and the layout follows.

Record	Field	Column Range
1	Title of Book	1–50
2	Year Book Published	1–4
2	Publisher of Book	6–30
2	City of Publisher	35–49

Resulting Data Set

Output 3.11 Data set
MYBOOKORDER

```
              Selected Books from My Book Order
     Obs    booktitle


       1    Retirement Planning for the Next Generation
       2    How to Cope with Busy Teenage Schedules
       3    Favorite Dogs Calendar 2003


     Obs    yearpublished      publisher      publishercity


       1         2002       Home Publishers     Chicago
       2         2002       Home Publishers     Chicago
       3         2002       Home Publishers     Chicago
```

Program

This DATA step uses INFILE statement options to read specific data lines from an external file.

Reviewing the external file, the data lines for Home Publishers start with data line 5 and continue to the tenth data line. These 6 data lines create three observations in MYBOOKORDER and are the ones that this DATA step reads.

```
data mybookorder;
   infile 'c:\readdata\example3_11.dat'
          truncover
```

Prevent the INPUT statement from moving to the next data line if the current data line is not as wide as the INPUT statement expects.

Begin reading the external file at the fifth data line.

```
          firstobs=5
```

Specify the last data line to read from the external file.

```
          obs=10;
```

Read the data with formatted input. Read two data lines per observation. Place the / line pointer control between the variables on the first data line and the variables on the second data line.

```
input booktitle $50. /
      yearpublished 4.
      @6 publisher $25.
      @35 publishercity $15.;
run;
proc print data=mybookorder;
   title 'Selected Books from My Book Order';
run;
```

A Closer Look

Determining When SAS Starts and Stops Processing Data When Specifying the FIRSTOBS= and OBS= Options

SAS sequentially reads each data line in an external file. For FIRSTOBS= values greater than 1, SAS does not start processing the data it reads until it reads the data line equal to the value assigned to the FIRSTOBS= option.

The number you specify with the OBS= option in the INFILE statement is the last data line that SAS reads from the external file.

The OBS= value is not the observation count. In this example, SAS reads six data lines, which results in three observations.

When there are fewer data lines in the external file than the value assigned to OBS=, the DATA step stops when it reaches the end of the external file.

Comparing FIRSTOBS= and OBS= as System Options to FIRSTOBS= and OBS= as Data Set or INFILE Statement Options

The FIRSTOBS= and OBS= options are also names for system options and data set options. They function similarly, but not always identically to the same-named options in the INFILE statement.

A difference is that when specified as INFILE or data set options, the options remain in effect only for the duration of the step. They supercede the settings for the corresponding system options. When multiple INFILE statements are present in the DATA step, the options only apply to the external file referenced by the INFILE statement that included the options. When the DATA step ends, the corresponding system options are again in effect.

When specified as system options, the values for FIRSTOBS= and OBS= remain in effect throughout the SAS session unless reset by an OPTIONS statement or by changing the option values in a windowing environment. The values for the system options restrict the observations read from a DATA set, and they also restrict the data lines read when reading data from an external file. They can be superseded temporarily as described in the previous paragraph.

If you modify this example so that the FIRSTOBS= and OBS= are specified as system options instead of INFILE statement options, the DATA step executes as before, but the PROC PRINT step does not produce a report. To produce a PROC PRINT report, data set MYBOOKORDER must contain at least five observations; the data set MYBOOKORDER contains only three observations.

The modified program in which the PROC PRINT step does not produce a report follows.

```
options firstobs=5 obs=10;
data mybookorder;
   infile 'c:\readdata\example3_11.dat' truncover;
   input booktitle $50. /
         yearpublished 4.
         @6 publisher $25.
         @35 publishercity $15.;
run;
proc print data=mybookorder;
   title 'Selected Books from My Book Order';
run;
```

A message in the SAS log for the PROC PRINT step confirms that the setting of the FIRSTOBS= option prevents production of the report.

```
1791  proc print data=mybookorder;
WARNING: FIRSTOBS option > number of observations in
         WORK.MYBOOKORDER.
1792    title 'Selected Books from My Book Order';
run;
```

Debugging and Testing Programs with the FIRSTOBS= and OBS= Options

Setting the FIRSTOBS= and OBS= options to appropriate values can be a way to find errors in your code. You can specifically test certain data lines or efficiently test your code on a subset of data.

Related Technique

The automatic variable _N_ tallies the number of iterations of the DATA step. Your DATA step statements can examine the value of _N_ to restrict the data lines read by the DATA step.

The DATA step creates _N_ automatically. This variable becomes part of the program data vector and SAS sets its value on each iteration of the DATA step. It exists for the duration of the DATA step; any SAS data sets created do not contain _N_. If you want to save the value of _N_ in a SAS data set, you must assign its value to a data set variable.

The DATA step that follows tests the value of _N_ so that it can restrict the data lines processed. This DATA step produces the same data set as shown in Output 3.11.

The first IF statement tells the DATA step to stop at its sixth iteration. The second IF statement tells the DATA step to output the data from the third, fourth, and fifth iterations only.

```
data mybookorder;
   infile 'c:\readdata\example3_11.dat' truncover;
   input booktitle $50. /
         yearpublished 4.
         @6 publisher $25.
         @35 publishercity $15.;

   if _n_ gt 5 then stop;
   if 3 le _n_ le 5;
run;
```

Example 3.12   Reading Special Missing Values

Goal

Read an external file where the missing values for numeric fields were generated for different reasons. The reasons are distinguished by using single characters instead of the default missing value of a period (.). The goal is to preserve the distinction among the missing values in the output data set.

Strategy

Specify the MISSING global statement to identify the single characters in the external file that represent numeric missing values.

Example Features

The relationship between the data lines of the external file and the observations of the data set is that

❐   one data line defines one observation.

Other features of this example include the

❐   MISSING statement.

External File

This external file contains the responses to a survey of customers at two pizza restaurants.

```
Pizaro's        Delivery 4 4 . N
Pizaro's        Delivery 3 R 3 N
Pizaro's        Dine-In  4 5 . 4
Pizaro's        Dine-In  4 R 2 5
Pizaro's        Delivery 4 R 2 N
Mamamia         Dine-In  1 . 2 R
Mamamia         Dine-In  R 3 4 4
Mamamia         Delivery 3 . . N
Mamamia         Delivery 2 3 3 N
Mamamia         Dine-In  R 3 4 4
Mamamia         Delivery 3 3 3 N
```

The data values are aligned in columns and the layout follows.

Field	Column Range
Name of Restaurant	1–15
Type of Service	17–24
Survey Question 1	26
Survey Question 2	28
Survey Question 3	30
Survey Question 4	32

The special missing value of R indicates the customer refused to answer the question. The special missing value N indicates the question is not applicable. The usual missing value representation of a period indicates the respondent ignored the question.

Resulting SAS Data Set

Output 3.11 PIZZASURVEY Data Set

```
                          Pizza Survey Results

     Obs  pizzaplace    type     pizzahot ontime courteous howsoonseated

       1  Pizaro's    Delivery      4       4        .          N
       2  Pizaro's    Delivery      3       R        3          N
       3  Pizaro's    Dine-In       4       5        .          4
       4  Pizaro's    Dine-In       4       R        2          5
       5  Pizaro's    Delivery      4       R        2          N
       6  Mamamia     Dine-In       1       .        2          R
       7  Mamamia     Dine-In       R       3        4          4
       8  Mamamia     Delivery      3       .        .          N
       9  Mamamia     Delivery      2       3        3          N
      10  Mamamia     Dine-In       R       3        4          4
      11  Mamamia     Delivery      3       3        3          N
```

Program

Identify the two special missing values defined in the external file.

Read the data with formatted input and list input.

This DATA step reads an external file where missing values have different meanings.

```
missing N R;

data pizzasurvey;
   infile 'c:\readdata\example3_12.dat';


   input pizzaplace $15. +1 type $8.
         pizzahot ontime courteous howsoonseated;

run;
proc print data=pizzasurvey;
  title 'Pizza Survey Results';
run;
```

⌕ A Closer Look

Specifying Special Missing Values

Valid special missing values include the 26 upper or lower case letters of the alphabet and the underscore(_). SAS does not distinguish between upper and lower case letters in the MISSING statement. For example, a special missing value of M has the same meaning as the special missing value of m.

Since the MISSING statement is a global SAS statement, the characters that you specify in the MISSING statement remain as special missing values throughout your SAS session.

When you sort a data set in ascending order by a numeric variable that contains special missing values, the special missing value of underscore (_) is smallest, the period (.) is next smallest, followed by all other special missing values. Negative numbers, zero, and positive numbers conclude the order.

Including Special Missing Values in SAS Statements

To represent a special missing value in a SAS statement, you must begin the value with a period and follow it by the special missing letter or underscore.

When special missing values are included in output, SAS displays only the letter or underscore.

The next program creates a format that can be applied to the two special missing values that were identified in the program above. The PROC PRINT output that follows presents the formatted data.

Represent a special missing value as a period followed by the special missing value when including it in a SAS statement.

```
missing N R;
proc format;
   value pizzafmt  .N='Not Applicable'
                   .R='Refused'
                   .='Missing';
run;
proc print data=pizzasurvey;
   title 'Pizza Survey Results';
   format pizzahot--howsoonseated pizzafmt.;
run;
```

The PROC PRINT output follows.

Output 3.12a PROC PRINT results

```
                         Pizza Survey Results

     Obs   pizzaplace    type         pizzahot      ontime

      1    Pizaro's      Deliver          4             4
      2    Pizaro's      Delivery         3       Refused
      3    Pizaro's      Dine-In          4             5
      4    Pizaro's      Dine-In          4       Refused
      5    Pizaro's      Delivery         4       Refused
      6    Mamamia       Dine-In          1       Missing
      7    Mamamia       Dine-In     Refused            3
      8    Mamamia       Delivery         3       Missing
      9    Mamamia       Delivery         2             3
     10    Mamamia       Dine-In     Refused            3
     11    Mamamia       Delivery         3             3


     Obs      courteous            howsoonseated

      1     Missing              Not Applicable
      2              3           Not Applicable
      3     Missing                           4
      4              2                         5
      5              2           Not Applicable
      6              2                  Refused
      7              4                         4
      8     Missing              Not Applicable
      9              3           Not Applicable
     10              4                         4
     11              3           Not Applicable
```

Example 3.13 Updating a SAS Data Set with Transactions Read from an External File

Goal

Update a master data set in place using values supplied by data from an external file. The data set is indexed by a variable that is also part of each data line in the external file.

Strategy

Write one DATA step that reads the external file and updates the SAS data set. Use the MODIFY statement with the KEY= option to update the data set. Verify that the master data set is indexed by the variable you want to identify as the key.

Specify in the DATA statement the name of the master data set, which is the data set you want to update. Follow the DATA statement with an INFILE statement that identifies the external file that contains the new information. Write an INPUT statement to read the key variable from the external file. Name this variable the same as the indexed variable in the master data set. Add a trailing at sign (@) to this INPUT statement so that more information can be read from this data line later in the DATA step.

Follow the INPUT statement with a MODIFY statement that includes the name of the master data set and the KEY= option. Set the KEY= option to the name of the index variable.

For each data line read from the external file, examine the results of the MODIFY statement to see if the key variable's value is in the data set. Test the value of the _IORC_ automatic variable to determine the success of the lookup.

If the lookup is successful, read the rest of the data line from the external file and overwrite the existing variable values with the new information. If the lookup is not successful, write a message to the SAS log. For a lookup that resulted in an undetermined error, write a message to the SAS log and stop the DATA step.

Example Features

The relationship between the data lines of the external file and the observations of the data set is that

❏ one data line modifies one observation.

The INPUT statement feature used in this example is

❏ trailing @

The INFILE statement options used in this example are the

❏ DELIMITER= option.

❏ TRUNCOVER option.

Other features of this example include the

❒ _IORC_ automatic variable

❒ MODIFY statement

❒ macro facility.

External File

Each data line in this external file contains information for a particular type of update of employee information.

```
39183~S~09/30/2002~$56,008.32~Network Analyst
39184~A~10/04/2002~76 East Parkway~Westville~MN~55126
39186~S~09/30/2002~$48,399.01~Senior Research Technician
39190~A~10/01/2002~3405 Turtle Lake Rd.~Shoreview~MN~55126
39185~S~09/30/2002~$59,039.77~Business Analyst
```

Data values are separated by a tilde (~).

The first field in the data line is the PERSONID, which is also the index variable in the SAS data set being updated. The data lines are not in order by PERSONID.

The second field indicates the type of update. Two types of updates are represented in this file: "A" for address and "S" for salary.

For an address data line, the data values after the A are

❒ date of address change (mm/dd/yyyy)

❒ street address

❒ city

❒ state

❒ zipcode.

For S type data lines, the data values after the S are

❒ date of salary update (mm/dd/yyyy)

❒ salary

❒ job title.

Existing SAS Data Set

This is an excerpt of a PROC PRINT of the CORP.EMPLOYEES data set presented in order by PERSONID. It includes the observations that should be updated with information from the external file. Note that there is no PERSONID=39186 in CORP.EMPLOYEES, but that a data line for this PERSONID exists in the external file containing the new data.

Output 3.13a CORP.EMPLOYEES Data Set Before Updating

```
               Employee Information Before Update

 Obs    personid    name                    address

  1      39182     Rice, Edward          4523 Klock Drive
  2      39183     Stevens, Sally        56 Thompson Lane
  3      39184     McDonald, Robert      4523 Hwy 35
  4      39185     Lewis, Martin         893 Maple Ave.
  5      39187     Little, Mary          12124 South St.
  6      39188     Lee, Richard          33 Bobolink Trail
  7      39189     Thomas, Ann           1113 Fletcher St.
  8      39190     West, Teri            422 8th Ave.


 Obs    city            state   zipcode  addressdate      salary

  1    Chain of Lakes    MN      55099   09/03/1988    $68,090.43
  2    Pleasantville     MN      55127   04/30/2000    $54,398.33
  3    Rivertown         MN      55999   05/24/1995    $83,729.98
  4    Chain of Lakes    MN      55099   03/15/1997    $57,928.54
  5    Roseville         MN      55100   02/28/1994    $43,231.78
  6    St. Croix         MN      55000   07/15/1990    $45,938.76
  7    Roseville         MN      55100   04/02/1997    $39,727.23
  8    Roseville         MN      55100   08/30/1999    $42,039.39


 Obs    salarydate      jobtitle

  1    12/31/2000      Sr. Analyst
  2    08/15/2000      Junior Network Analyst
  3    04/30/2001      Manager
  4    09/15/2001      Business Associate
  5    01/15/2002      Editor
  6    06/15/2002      Research Technician III
  7    08/31/2001      Senior Secretary
  8    08/31/2001      Marketing Analyst I
```

Resulting Data Set

This PROC PRINT shows the changes made to the observations in the CORP.EMPLOYEES data set.

Output 3.13b CORP.EMPLOYEES Data Set After Update

```
                     Employee Information After Update

     Obs    personid   name                        address

      1      39182     Rice, Edward           4523 Klock Drive
      2      39183     Stevens, Sally         56 Thompson Lane
      3      39184     McDonald, Robert       76 East Parkway
      4      39185     Lewis, Martin          893 Maple Ave.
      5      39187     Little, Mary           12124 South St.
      6      39188     Lee, Richard           33 Bobolink Trail
      7      39189     Thomas, Ann            1113 Fletcher St.
      8      39190     West, Teri             3405 Turtle Lake Rd.


     Obs    city             state   zipcode   addressdate      salary

      1    Chain of Lakes     MN      55099    09/03/1988    $68,090.43
      2    Pleasantville      MN      55127    04/30/2000    $56,008.32
      3    Westville          MN      55126    10/04/2002    $83,729.98
      4    Chain of Lakes     MN      55099    03/15/1997    $59,039.77
      5    Roseville          MN      55100    02/28/1994    $43,231.78
      6    St. Croix          MN      55000    07/15/1990    $45,938.76
      7    Roseville          MN      55100    04/02/1997    $39,727.23
      8    Shoreview          MN      55126    10/01/2002    $42,039.39


     Obs    salarydate      jobtitle

      1     12/31/2000     Sr. Analyst
      2     09/30/2002     Network Analyst
      3     04/30/2001     Manager
      4     09/30/2002     Business Analyst
      5     01/15/2002     Editor
      6     06/15/2002     Research Technician III
      7     08/31/2001     Senior Secretary
      8     08/31/2001     Marketing Analyst I
```

Program

This DATA step modifies a data set with information read from an external file. The SAS data set is indexed and the index variable is included in each data line.

Specify the name of the data set you want to modify, which can be referred to as the master data set.

```
data corp.employees;
```

Identify the external file that contains the new information.

```
    infile 'c:\readdata\example3_13.dat'
```

Specify the delimiter between data values.

```
            delimiter='~'
```

Prevent the INPUT statement from moving to the next data line if the current data line is not as wide as the INPUT statement expects.

```
            truncover;
```

Read the value for the key. Make sure that the name specified here is the same as the name of the index variable in the data set you want to modify.

```
    input personid
```

Keep the current data line in the input buffer so that further processing can determine how to input the rest of the data line.

```
        @;
```

Indicate the name of the master data set.

```
    modify corp.employees
```

Specify the name of the variable that links the data set and the data in the external file.

```
            key=personid;
```

Evaluate the automatic variable, IORC_, which is the numeric return code of the most recently executed MODIFY or SET statement that included the KEY= option.

```
    select (_iorc_);
```

Specify in the SELECT block the actions to take based on the value of _IORC_.

Test the value of the _SOK mnemonic that represents that a match was successfully made. Apply the SYSRC macro program to this value.

```
        when (%sysrc(_sok)) do;
```

Read the record type of the data line that indicates the content of the rest of the line.

```
input updatetype $
```

Keep the current data line in the input buffer so that further processing can determine how to input the rest of the data line.

```
                @;
```

Read the address information with modified list input, formatted input, and list input.

```
if updatetype='A' then do;
  input addressdate : mmddyy10.
        address : $30.
        city    : $20.
        state     $2.
        zipcode;
```

Replace the current variable values in the CORP.EMPLOYEES data set with the information just read.

```
  replace;
end;
```

Read the salary information with modified list input.

```
else if updatetype='S' then do;
  input salarydate : mmddyy10.
        salary : comma10.2
        jobtitle : $25.;
```

Replace the current variable values in the master data set with the information just read.

```
  replace;
end;
```

Write a note to the SAS log indicating that an unknown update type was identified. Do not include a REPLACE statement in this block since there is no information to update.

```
else do;
  put '***** Update Type not A or S for ' personid;
end;
end;
```

Test the value of the _DSENOM mnemonic that represents when no matching observation was found. Apply the SYSRC macro program to this value.

```
when (%sysrc(_dsenom)) do;
```

Write a message to the SAS log displaying the value of PERSONID from the unmatched data line in the external file.

```
put '***** Person ID Not Found: ' personid;
```

**Reset the value of the
automatic variable, _ERROR_,
to 0 that SAS set to 1 when the
match could not be made.**
Prevent the display of the input
data line and the variable
values for the observation
where SAS determined that a
match could not be made by
resetting the value of
ERROR to 0 that SAS had
set to 1.

```
          _error_=0;
      end;
```

**For all other values of _IORC_,
write a message to the SAS log
that displays the value of the
automatic variable _IORC_
and the contents of the input
buffer as represented by the
automatic variable, _INFILE_.**

```
    otherwise do;
       put '***** Unexpected Error: ' _iorc_= _infile_;
```

**Stop executing the DATA step
because of this unknown
condition.**

```
       stop;
      end;
    end;
  end;
run;
```

🔍 **A Closer Look**

Reviewing the Messages and Notes from this Example

The goal of this example is to update observations in a master data set with information provided in an external file. There are five data lines in the external file. SAS does not find a match for the third data line.

When viewing the messages and notes produced by this example's DATA step, you will see the message generated that indicates that a match was not found for the third data line. Additionally, the notes indicate that the DATA step updated four observations.

A copy of the messages and notes follows.

```
***** Person ID Not Found: 39186
NOTE: 5 records were read from the infile
      'c:\readdata\example3_13.dat'.
      The minimum record length was 45.
      The maximum record length was 58.
NOTE: The data set WORK.EMPLOYEES has been updated.  There
      Were 4 observations rewritten, 0 observations added
      and 0 observations deleted.
NOTE: DATA statement used:
      real time           0.22 seconds
```

Understanding the _IORC_ Automatic Variable and the SYSRC Macro Program

Your DATA step automatically creates the automatic variable _IORC_ when you use the KEY= option with the MODIFY statement or the SET statement. The value of _IORC_ is a numeric return code that indicates the status of the most recently executed MODIFY or SET statement that included the KEY= option. Testing the value of _IORC_ can determine the success of the execution of the MODIFY or SET statement and you can then direct execution of code based on the value of _IORC_.

The values of _IORC_ may change with different versions of SAS. To make your code independent of the SAS version, SAS processes a mnemonic that in turn finds the associated return code for your current system.

The SYSRC macro program translates the mnemonic into the return code for your system. Its one argument is a mnemonic representing a condition that SAS can detect when executing your MODIFY or SET statement that includes the KEY= option. The two mnemonics tested in this example are _SOK and _DSENOM.

Where to Go from Here

Refer to *SAS Language Reference: Dictionary* for more information on the SET and MODIFY statements.

Refer to *Combining and Modifying SAS Data Sets: Examples* for examples of using the MODIFY statement with the KEY= option. This reference also more fully describes the _IORC_ automatic variable and the SYSRC macro program.

Refer to *SAS Macro Language: Reference* for more information on how to apply the SYSRC macro program.

Example 3.14 Reading Nonstandard Numeric Data Values and Converting Them to Standard Numeric Data Values by Examining the Data Value

Goal

Read an external file where a field contains nonstandard numeric data. Determine the informat with which to read the value by examining the value with DATA step statements.

Strategy

Read the nonstandard numeric field as character data. Use IF-THEN statements and functions to determine the informat to use to read the data. Apply the informat to the character value with the INPUT function to create a standard numeric value.

Example Features

The relationship between the data lines of the external file and the observations of the data set is that

❏ one data line defines one observation.

The INFILE statement option used in this example is the

❏ TRUNCOVER option.

Other features of this example include

❏ nonstandard numeric data

❏ INPUT function.

External File

The data lines in this external file contain several nonstandard and standard numeric values.

```
10:00
01/01/00
123456
35.8%
1:32PM
3-31-2002
'0A'x
January 30, 1998
99.765
```

This external file contains one field per data line.

All values but those on data lines 3 and 9 are nonstandard numeric data.

Conversion information for the data type on data line 8 is not included in the program.

Resulting Data set

Output 3.14 VALUES Data Set

```
          Nonstandard and Standard Data Values

     Obs      nonstdvalue        stdnum

      1       10:00            36000.00
      2       01/01/00         14610.00
      3       123456          123456.00
      4       35.8%                0.36
      5       1:32PM           48720.00
      6       3-31-2002        15430.00
      7       '0A'x               10.00
      8       January 30           .
      9       99.765              99.77
```

Program

This DATA step reads nonstandard numeric data values, looks for specific characters in the data values, and then converts the nonstandard data values to standard numeric data values by applying informats appropriate to the characters found in the data value.

The DATA step can process four different types of nonstandard numeric data: time, date, percent, and hexadecimal. In addition, if the value is already in standard numeric format, the program converts the character representation to numeric. If a value does not fit into any of the expected types of data, the DATA step writes a message to the SAS log.

```sas
data values;
   infile 'c:\readdata\example3_14.dat'
         truncover;
```

Prevent the INPUT statement from moving to the next data line if the current data line is not as wide as the INPUT statement expects.

```sas
   input nonstdvalue $10.;
```

Write a series of IF-THEN-ELSE statements that look for specific characters in the variable NONSTDVALUE.

```sas
   /* Read time value */
   if index(nonstdvalue,':') > 1 then
```

Apply the appropriate numeric information to the current value of NONSTDVALUE and convert the value to numeric by applying the INPUT function.

```
      stdnum=input(nonstdvalue,time10.);

   /* Read date value */
   else if index(nonstdvalue,'/') > 0 or
          index(nonstdvalue,'-') > 0 then
      stdnum=input(nonstdvalue,mmddyy10.);

   /* Read percents */
   else if index(nonstdvalue,'%') > 0 then
      stdnum=input(nonstdvalue,percent6.1);
```

Remove the hexadecimal constant representation from NONSTDVALUE. Apply the informat to what remains.

```
   /* Read hex values */
   else if index(nonstdvalue,"'x") > 0 then
      stdnum=input(compress(nonstdvalue,"'x"),hex10.);

   /* Value is already standard numeric */
   else if verify(nonstdvalue,'0123456789. ')=0 then
      stdnum=input(nonstdvalue,10.);
```

Write a message to the SAS log when the type of nonstandard numeric data cannot be determined.

```
   /* Value not accounted for in tests above */
   else put 'Unspecified data type for: ' nonstdvalue;
run;
proc print data=values;
   title 'Nonstandard and Standard Data Values';
run;
```

A Closer Look

Understanding Nonstandard Data

Nonstandard data are numeric values that contain special characters or have a representation different from numbers. To define them as numeric values, read them with an informat.

Examples of nonstandard data include numeric values that contain commas, dollar signs, or blanks; date and time values; and hexadecmimal and binary values.

Understanding the INPUT Function

This program illustrates a way to reread data values after determining information about the values. The INPUT function gives you the capability to reinterpret a value after the INPUT statement has read the value.

This program uses the INPUT function to apply an informat to a data value. Either a character or numeric informat can be an argument to this function. The type of the data value that results is the same type as the informat.

Two other INPUT functions are the INPUTN and INPUTC functions. The results of the INPUTN function are numeric while the results of the INPUTC function are character.

Related Technique

Another way of examining a data value and then rereading it is to hold the data line in the input buffer throughout the iteration of the DATA step. The trailing @ added to the INPUT statement keeps a data line in the input buffer so that the data line can be reread.

The following DATA step produces the same data set as shown in 3.14. It includes a trailing @ in the first INPUT statement and does not apply the INPUT function.

This DATA step is more restrictive in the hexadecimal values that it can process than the previous DATA step. It assumes that the hexadecimal value starts in column 2 and is only 2 bytes wide. Using the statements from the previous DATA step that process hexadecimal values may be a better choice.

```
data values;
   infile 'c:\readdata\example3_14.dat'
           truncover;

   input nonstdvalue $10. @;
```

Position the pointer back to column 1 to reread the data value.

```
   /* Read time value */
   if index(nonstdvalue,':') > 1 then
        input @1 stdnum time10.;

   /* Read date value */
   else if index(nonstdvalue,'/') > 0 or
           index(nonstdvalue,'-') > 0 then
        input @1 stdnum mmddyy10.;

   /* Read percents */
   else if index(nonstdvalue,'%') > 0 then
     input @1 stdnum percent6.1;

   /* Read hex values */
   else if index(nonstdvalue,"'x") > 0 then do;
     input @2 stdnum hex2.;
   end;

   /* Value is already standard numeric */
   else if verify(nonstdvalue,'0123456789. ')=0 then
     input @1 stdnum 10.;

   /* Value not accounted for in tests above */
   else put 'Unspecified data type for: ' nonstdvalue;
run;
```

Related Technique

User-defined informats can also be arguments to the INPUT function. This next example defines an informat that is referenced by the INPUT function.

The INPUT statement reads in a character representation of the ages of four children. The variable NUMAGE is a numeric representation of the age range as defined by the $AGEGRP informat.

```
proc format;
   invalue $agegrp  '0-4'=4
                    '5-9'=7
                    '10-14'=10
                    other=0;
run;
data ages;
   infile datalines truncover;
   input @1 name $10. @12 agerange $5.;

   length numage 8;

   numage=input(agerange,$agegrp.);
datalines;
Emily       0-4
Andrea      10-14
Louise      15-19
Marie       5-9
;;;;
proc print data=ages;
   title 'Ages';
run;
```

Define NUMAGE as a numeric field. If NUMAGE was not defined as numeric, it would be defined as character at execution of the NUMAGE= assignment statement.

The PROC PRINT output for this program follows.

Example 3.14a AGES SAS Data Set

```
                            Ages

        Obs       name      agerange     numage

         1        Emily       0-4          4
         2        Andrea      10-14        10
         3        Louise      15-19        0
         4        Marie       5-9          7
```

CHAPTER 4
OPERATING SYSTEM SPECIFIC FEATURES WHEN READING EXTERNAL FILES

Introduction

This chapter presents examples specific to the operating system under which SAS is reading your external file.

You can adapt some of the examples to run on different operating systems and the modifications to do this are identified.

The programs in this chapter also provide you with additional examples of writing DATA steps to read raw data.

Example Overview

These tables present overviews of the features of the examples in this chapter.

Operating System	4.1	4.2	4.3	4.4	4.5	4.6	4.7	4.8	4.9	4.10	4.11	4.12	4.13	4.14	4.15	4.16
Directory-based system (OpenVMS, UNIX, Windows)	●	●	●	●	●	●			●	●	●	●		●		●
Mainframe (OS/390)		●	●	●	●	●	●	●		●		●	●		●	

INFILE Statement Features	4.1	4.2	4.3	4.4	4.5	4.6	4.7	4.8	4.9	4.10	4.11	4.12	4.13	4.14		
Create a variable that detects when SAS reads the last data line from an external file (END=)							●				●					
Name a statement label that SAS directs processing to when it reaches the end of the external file (EOF=)										●						
Define a variable that SAS sets to the VSAM logical error code (FEEDBACK=)								●								
Specify the variable that determines which external file SAS is to read (FILEVAR=)							●				●					
Define a variable that serves as a key to an indexed data set (KEY=)								●								
Specify the length of the input record (LRECL=)	●								●							
Ignore carriage-control characters in the first byte of the external file (PRINT)													●			
Specify the format of the input record (RECFM)											●	●				
Prevent SAS from moving to a new input line when the current input line is not as wide as expected (TRUNCOVER)	●			●								●	●			
VSAM data set processing (VSAM)								●								

INPUT Statement Features	4.1	4.2	4.3	4.4	4.5	4.6	4.7	4.8	4.9	4.10	4.11	4.12	4.13	4.14	4.15	4.16
Reread a data line within an iteration of the DATA step (trailing @)								●				●				
Read multiple observations from one data line (double trailing @ (@@))										●				●		
Read variable-length variables($VARYING informat)										●						
Other Features	4.1	4.2	4.3	4.4	4.5	4.6	4.7	4.8	4.9	4.10	4.11	4.12	4.13	4.14		
Aggregate storage			●													
Concatenated external files		●														
Environment variables				●												
FILENAME Statement Specifications		●	●								●					
Nonstandard data values						●			●				●			
Partitioned data sets (OS/390)					●		●									
PROC SOURCE							●									
Processing magnetic tapes														●	●	●
SAS/CONNECT						●			●							
SAS functions to obtain information about external files					●											
VSAM data set processing								●								

Example 4.1   Directory-based Systems: Reading Wide Records

Goal

Read an external file whose record length is longer than the SAS default record length. The external file is stored on a directory-based system such as Windows. Assume SAS is executing on a directory-based system.

Strategy

Specify the logical record length of the external file with the LRECL= option in the INFILE statement. Set this value to at least the longest record length in the external file.

Include the TRUNCOVER option in the INFILE statement so that SAS does not move to the next data line if the current one does not have data out to the length specified in the LRECL= option.

Example Features

This example can execute under the following operating systems:

❑ directory-based systems (OpenVMS, UNIX, Windows).

The INFILE statement options used in this example are

❑ LRECL= option

❑ TRUNCOVER option.

External File

This external file contains information about three students who have taken SAS classes.

The representation of the external file is shown at the right, 50 columns at a time.

```
----+----1----+----2----+----3----+----4----+----5
Smith               Susan          Rose
Lewis               Carol          Ann
Morris              Mark           D.
----+----6----+----7----+----8----+----9----+----0
   ABC Consulting Inc.             300 West Shore D
   HiTech Company                  One HiTech Place
   Professional Consultants        95 Oak Forest Wa
         1         1         1         1         1
----+----1----+----2----+----3----+----4----+----5
rive           Suite 101                       Mapl
               Mailstop 3028                    High
y              Building 32                      Howa
         1         1         1         1         2
----+----6----+----7----+----8----+----9----+----0
etown          Massachusetts       02999-9999 0
land           Illinois            60000-9999 0
rd             North Carolina      27000-9999 0
         2         2         2         2         2
----+----1----+----2----+----3----+----4----+----5
5/13/2002 SAS Basics I                      06/17/200
1/14/2002 Advanced DATA Step Programming
1/14/2002 Advanced DATA Step Programming 03/04/200
         2         2         2         2         3
----+----6----+----7----+----8----+----9----+----0
2 Report-Writing Fundamentals     09/25/2002 Statis
2 SAS Macro Programming
         3         3
----+----1----+----2----
tical Analysis II
```

Each data line contains a student's name, address, and SAS classes that the student has attended. Up to three SAS classes can be recorded for a student. The maximum length that a record can be in this file is 324 bytes.

The data values are aligned in columns and the layout follows.

Field	Column Range
Last name	1–20
First name	22–36
Middle name	38–52
Company name	54–83
Address line 1	85–114
Address line 2	116–145
City	147–166
State	168–187
Zip code	189–198
Date of first class	200–209
Name of first class	211–240
Date of second class	242–251
Name of second class	253–282
Date of third class	284–293
Name of third class	295–324

Resulting Data Set

Output 4.1 PROC PRINT of SASSTUDENTS Data Set

```
                    SAS Students

Obs    lastname  firstname  middlename    company

 1      Smith      Susan       Rose       ABC Consulting Inc.
 2      Lewis      Carol       Ann        HiTech Company
 3      Morris     Mark        D.         Professional Consultants


Obs       address1              address2       city          state

 1    300 West Shore Drive    Suite 101      Mapletown     Massachusetts
 2    One HiTech Place        Mailstop 3028  Highland      Illinois
 3    95 Oak Forest Way       Building 32    Howard        North Carolina
```

Output 4.1 PROC PRINT of SASSTUDENTS Data Set (continued)

```
    Obs    zip        classdate1    classname1


     1  02999-9999   05/13/2002    SAS Basics I
     2  60000-9999   01/14/2002    Advanced DATA Step Programming
     3  27000-9999   01/14/2002    Advanced DATA Step Programming


   Obs classdate2              classname2              classdate3


    1  06/17/2002     Report-Writing Fundamentals   09/25/2002
    2       .                                            .
    3  03/04/2002     SAS Macro Programming               .


   Obs          classname3


    1  Statistical Analysis II
    2
    3
```

Program

This DATA step reads an external file where the data in a data line can extend beyond the SAS default record length. The program executes under SAS for Windows.

```
data sasstudents;
   infile 'c:\readdata\example4_1.dat'
```

Set the value of the LRECL= option to the record length of the external file.

```
   lrecl=324
```

Prevent the INPUT statement from moving to the next data line if the current data line is not as wide as the INPUT statement expects.

```
   truncover;
```

Read the data with column input and formatted input.

```
input lastname    $ 1-20
      firstname   $ 22-36
      middlename  $ 38-52
      company     $ 54-83
      address1    $ 85-114
      address2    $ 116-145
      city        $ 147-166
      state       $ 168-187
      zip         $ 189-198
      @200 classdate1 mmddyy10.
      classname1 $ 211-240
```

```
                              @242 classdate2 mmddyy10.
                              classname2 $ 253-282
                              @284 classdate3 mmddyy10.
                              classname3 $ 295-324;

                    format classdate1-classdate3 mmddyy10.;
               run;
               proc print data=sasstudents;
                    title 'SAS Students';
               run;
```

🔍 A Closer Look

Interpreting the SAS Log when Reading an External File whose Record Length is Greater than the Default and the LRECL= or TRUNCOVER or Both Options Have Been Omitted

When your record length is greater than the default and you omit the LRECL= or TRUNCOVER options or both from the INFILE statement, you may see a variety of error messages and notes written to the SAS log. These messages result from SAS moving to the next input data line to continue reading data for an observation if the data in the current data line is not as wide as specified on the INPUT statement.

Some of the messages that you may see follow.

```
NOTE: Invalid data for varname.


NOTE: LOST CARD.


NOTE: One or more lines were truncated.


NOTE: SAS went to a new line when INPUT statement
      reached past the end of a line.
```

Specifying a Record Length

When specifying a record length, you may need to refer to SAS documentation for your operating system to determine the default record length and the maximum record length.

Under SAS for Windows, if you do not specify a record length, SAS defaults to a record length of 256 bytes. The maximum record length allowed under SAS for Windows is 1,048,576.

Where to Go From Here

For a more complete discussion on the TRUNCOVER INFILE statement option and related options, see Example 2.11.

For a discussion of file structures on directory based systems, refer to TS-642, "Reading EBCDIC Files on ASCII Systems."

Example 4.2 Reading from Multiple External Files That Have the Same Layout

Goal

Read from several external files in one DATA step. The external files have the same layout.

Strategy

Write one FILENAME statement and specify the external files as concatenated files in the FILENAME statement. Specify this FILENAME statement appropriately for your operating system. Write one DATA step that has one INFILE statement that references the fileref defined in the FILENAME statement.

Example Features

This example can execute under the following operating systems:

❑ directory-based system (OpenVMS, UNIX, Windows)

❑ mainframe (OS/390).

Other features of this example include:

❑ concatenated external files

❑ FILENAME statement specifications.

External File 1

This file contains the race times for the Green team.

```
Mark S.        Green 12 12 15
Brad Y.        Green 13 11 59
Alex C.        Green 14 13 43
Ryan C.        Green 12 15 15
Tom B.         Green 14 10 30
Todd C.        Green 14 9  4
Dan Y.         Green 13 12 11
Jason L.       Green 12 14 5
```

External File 2

This file contains the race times for the Blue team.

```
Scott B.       Blue  14 9  50
Mark B.        Blue  13 13 1
Matthew S.     Blue  13 12 39
Colin K.       Blue  12 12 25
Joe K.         Blue  12 13 57
Joel O.        Blue  13 12 32
Mike C.        Blue  14 11 13
Craig A.       Blue  13 13 51
```

Each data line contains information about one runner. The data values are aligned in columns and the layout follows.

Field	Column Range
Runner's name	1–12
Team	14–18
Runner's age	20–21
Runner's time minutes part	23–24
Runner's time seconds part	26–27

Resulting Data Set

The order of the observations shows that SAS reads the data for the Green team first.

Output 4.2 PROC PRINT of RACETIMES Data Set

```
                     Runners and Race Times

   Obs    name        team      age    minutes    seconds

    1    Mark S.      Green      12       12         15
    2    Brad Y.      Green      13       11         59
    3    Alex C.      Green      14       13         43
    4    Ryan C.      Green      12       15         15
    5    Tom B.       Green      14       10         30
    6    Todd C.      Green      14        9          4
    7    Dan Y.       Green      13       12         11
    8    Jason L.     Green      12       14          5
    9    Scott B.     Blue       14        9         50
   10    Mark B.      Blue       13       13          1
   11    Matthew S    Blue       13       12         39
   12    Colin K.     Blue       12       12         25
   13    Joe K.       Blue       12       13         57
   14    Joel O.      Blue       13       12         32
   15    Mike C.      Blue       14       11         13
   16    Craig A.     Blue       13       13         51
```

Program

List in the FILENAME statement all the names of the external files that the DATA step should read. Enclose the list of filenames in parentheses and separate the filenames with a comma. Write the FILENAME statement in the form required for your operating system.

Specify the fileref that points to the list of external files that the DATA step should read.

Write one INPUT statement to read the external files. Read these specific external files with formatted input.

This DATA step reads the two external files listed in the FILENAME statement. The external files are stored on a Windows system and the DATA step executes on a Windows system.

```
filename twofiles ('c:\books\readdata\example4_2.dat',
                   'c:\books\readdata\ example4_2b.dat');
```

```
data racetimes;
   infile twofiles;

   input @1 name $12. @14 team $5. @20 age 2.
         @23 minutes 2. @26 seconds 2.;
run;
proc print data=racetimes;
   title 'Runners and Race Times';
run;
```

System Specific Information

The way you write your FILENAME statement depends on the requirements of your operating system. The program above runs under Windows. Examples of FILENAME statements for similarly named external files under other operating systems follow.

Open VMS

```
filename twofiles ('[readdata]example4_2.dat',
                   '[readdata]example4_2b.dat');
```

OS/390

From within a SAS session:

```
filename twofiles ('readdata.ex4_2',
                   'readdata.ex4_2b');
```

Submitted through JCL:

```
//TWOFILES DD DSN=READDATA.EX4_2,DISP=SHR,
//         DD DSN=READDATA.EX4_2B,DISP=SHR
```

UNIX

```
filename twofiles ('/readdata/example4_2',
                   '/readdata/example4_1b');
```

A Closer Look

Differentiating Between Concatenated External Files and Aggregate Storage

The concepts of defining a fileref to refer to several files and defining a fileref to refer to several storage locations are similar. Both provide you with the potential to reduce the amount of coding you do and to more efficiently access files in your DATA steps.

Determining which technique to use depends on your needs.

❑ Define your FILENAME statement with concatenated external files if you need to read several external files in one DATA step.

❑ Define your FILENAME statement as an aggregate storage location if you need to read one external file that may be in one of a group of directories.

Example 4.3 presents an example of aggregating storage locations in which the DATA step searches the locations and reads the first occurrence of the specified external file.

Related Technique

When you use the FILEVAR= option in the INFILE statement, you can read multiple external files within one DATA step. The value specified for the FILEVAR= option is the name of a variable whose values are filenames.

Refer to examples 4.7 and 4.11 for DATA steps that use the FILEVAR= option in the INFILE statement.

Example 4.3 Reading an External File That Is in One of Several Directories

Goal

Read an external file that is in one of a set of known directories.

Strategy

Write one FILENAME statement specifying the directories in which the external file can be found as an aggregate storage location. Write the FILENAME statement as required for your operating system. In the INFILE statement, reference the fileref that identifies the aggregate storage location. Follow the fileref with the external filename enclosed in parentheses.

Example Features

This example can execute under the following operating systems:

❏ directory-based systems (OpenVMS, UNIX, Windows)

❏ mainframe (OS/390).

Other features of this example include

❏ aggregate storage

❏ FILENAME statement specifications.

External File

This external file contains information about the number of trees on a specific plot of land.

```
Tilia americana          Basswood         5
Prunus serotina          Black Cherry   121
Quercus macrocapra       Bur Oak          2
Fraxinus pennsylvanica   Green Ash       87
Ostyra virginiana        Ironwood        42
Amelanchier arborea      Juneberry       32
Betula papyrifera        Paper Birch      1
Quercus rubra            Red Oak         39
Acer saccharinum         Silver Maple     2
Acer saccharum           Sugar Maple      8
Quercus alba             White Oak       10
```

Each data line records the number of trees per species in a plot of land. The data values are aligned in columns and the layout follows.

Field	Column Range
Scientific name of the tree	1–22
Common name of the tree	25–35
Number of trees	39–42

Output 4.3 TREES Data Set

```
                         Trees in Plot

       Obs    scientific                 tree          count

         1    Tilia americana            Basswood          5
         2    Prunus serotina            Black Cherry    121
         3    Quercus macrocapra         Bur Oak           2
         4    Fraxinus pennsylvanica     Green Ash        87
         5    Ostyra virginiana          Ironwood         42
         6    Amelanchier arborea        Juneberry        32
         7    Betula papyrifera          Paper Birch       1
         8    Quercus rubra              Red Oak          39
         9    Acer saccharinum           Silver Maple      2
        10    Acer saccharum             Sugar Maple       8
        11    Quercus alba               White Oak        10
```

Program

This program reads an external file that is in one of a set of known directories. It runs unders Windows.

Specify the directories in which the external file can be found.
Assign this aggregate location to the fileref TREES. Separate the directories with a comma. Enclose the list in parentheses. Write the FILENAME statement in the form required for your operating system.

```
filename trees ('c:\readdata','d:\readdata');
```

Specify the fileref that points to the aggregate storage location.
Follow the fileref with the name of the external data file and enclose the filename with parentheses.

```
data trees;
   infile trees(trees2002.dat);
```

Read the data with formatted input.

```
   input @1  scientific  $22.
         @25 tree        $11.
         @39 count       3.;
run;
proc print data=trees;
   title 'Trees in Plot';
run;
```

A Closer Look

Understanding How SAS Searches for an External File in an Aggregate Location

An INFILE statement that refers to an external file in an aggregate location only reads the first occurrence of the external file. In this example, if TREES2002.DAT existed in both directories, the DATA step would only read the file found in the first directory in the list, C:\READDATA.

Differentiating Between Concatenated External Files and Aggregate Storage

Refer to "A Closer Look" in Example 4.2 for a comparison of defining a fileref to refer to several files and defining a fileref to refer to several storage locations.

See Example 4.2 for an example of concatenating external files to be read as though the files are one.

Viewing the FILENAME Window

The following display shows how SAS defines the fileref for TREES in this example. Note that there are two entries for TREES, one for each of the two directories. Issue the FILENAME command in the command window to display the FILENAME window.

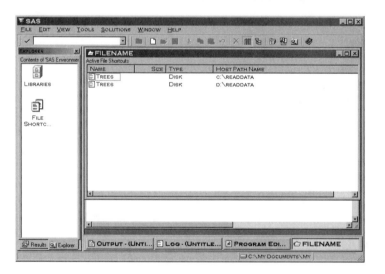

System-specific Information

The way you write your FILENAME statement depends on the requirements of your operating system. The program above runs under Windows. Examples of FILENAME and INFILE statements for similarly named directories and external files under other operating systems follow.

Open VMS

```
filename trees ('[readone]', '[readtwo]');
```

The INFILE statement would look like this:

```
infile trees(trees2002.dat);
```

OS/390

From within a SAS session:

The two entries in the FILENAME statement represent partitioned data sets.

```
filename trees ('myid.trees.readone(trees2002)',
                'myid.trees.readtwo(trees2002)');
```

Submitted through JCL:

```
//TREES      DD DSN=MYID.TREES.READONE(TREES2002),DISP=SHR
//           DD DSN=MYID.TREES.READTWO(TREES2002),DISP=SHR
```

The INFILE statement in both situations would look like this:

```
infile trees(trees2002);
```

Note that Example 4.8 presents an example of reading from a PDS.

UNIX

```
filename trees ('/readone/',
                '/readtwo/');
```

The INFILE statement would look like this:

```
infile trees(trees2002);
```

Example 4.4 Specifying the Name of an External File When Starting a SAS Session

Goal

Create a SAS data set by reading an external file where the external file was identified when starting a SAS session.

Strategy

Define an environment variable when the SAS session starts that points to the external file. Use the environment variable name as the fileref in the INFILE statement in the DATA step that reads the external file.

Example Features

This example can execute under the following operating systems:

❑ directory-based systems (OpenVMS, UNIX, Windows)

❑ mainframe (OS/390).

The INFILE statement option used in this example is

❑ TRUNCOVER option.

Other features of this example include:

❑ environment variables.

External File

This external file contains weekly travel information for several employees.

```
HGH 10/06/2002 3 Chicago
TIW 10/06/2002 1 Atlanta
RON 10/07/2002 1 Dallas
PAA 10/07/2002 3 San Francisco
NBS 10/08/2002 1 Cleveland
EMB 10/08/2002 2 NYC
JAZ 10/09/2002 3 Portland OR
KBB 10/10/2002 1 Boston
```

The data values are aligned in columns and the layout follows.

Field	Column Range
Employee's initials	1–3
Departure date	5–14
Duration of travel	16
Destination	18–42

Resulting Data Set

Output 4.4 PROC PRINT of WEEKLYTRAVEL Data Set

```
                  This Week's Travel Schedule


   Obs      empinits    departure    days     destination

    1         HGH       10/06/2002     3       Chicago
    2         TIW       10/06/2002     1       Atlanta
    3         RON       10/07/2002     1       Dallas
    4         PAA       10/07/2002     3       San Francisco
    5         NBS       10/08/2002     1       Cleveland
    6         EMB       10/08/2002     2       NYC
    7         JAZ       10/09/2002     3       Portland OR
    8         KBB       10/10/2002     1       Boston
```

Program

This program reads an external file that has been identified by an environment variable at the start of the SAS session.

The code shown runs under Windows.

Under Windows and Version 8 of SAS, place the definition of your environment variable in your SASV8.CFG file. Place this definition in your CONFIG.SAS file if you are a Version 6 user. Under either Version 8 or Version 6, use the SET command to associate an environment variable with an external file.

The name of the environment variable in this example is THISWEEK and the name of the external file is
`c:\readdata\example4_4.dat`.

At the top of either your SASV8.CFG or your CONFIG.SAS file, add the following line:

```
-set thisweek c:\readdata\example4_4.dat
```

If you instead invoke SAS from a shortcut on your Windows desktop, add the same SET command to the target properties.

The DATA step to read the external file identified by an environment variable follows.

```
data weeklytravel;
   infile thisweek truncover;
```

Place the environment variable name as the fileref in the INFILE statement.

Read the data with formatted input.

```
   input @1   empinits $3.
         @5   departure mmddyy10.
         @16  days 1.
         @18  destination $25.;
   format departure mmddyy10.;
run;
```

```
proc print data=weeklytravel;
  title 'This Week''s Travel Schedule';
run;
```

A Closer Look

Verifying the Assignment of Environment Variables

At the start of your SAS session, if you view the FILENAME window before you submit a reference to your environment variable, you will not find a fileref defined for your environment variable.

Once you submit a program that references the environment variable, you will be able to view the definition of the environment variable in the FILENAME window. The following was displayed after the DATA step above was submitted. It shows the assignment of the environment variable to the external file.

Related Technique

Under Windows, you can also define environment variables with the Windows SET command. This SET command, however, must be placed in the AUTOEXEC.BAT file that is invoked when Windows starts. Alternatively, it may be specified in the MS-DOS window that invokes your SAS session. The form of the Windows SET command follows.

```
SET THISWEEK=C:\READDATA\EXAMPLE4_4.DAT
```

System-specific Information

OS/390

Many sites invoke SAS interactively with a CLIST. You may need to check with your technical support group to determine how to pass an environment variable to SAS when you start your session.

UNIX

The UNIX operating system allows you to define environment variables that pass the name of an external file to your SAS session at the time your session starts.

A way to define the environment variable under the Korn shell is shown in the following command:

```
export THISWEEK=/readdata/example4_4.dat
```

Under UNIX, you can also define an environment variable after your SAS session starts. The following SAS statement submitted within your SAS session defines the THISWEEK environment variable:

```
x setenv THISWEEK /readdata/example4_4.dat;
```

Example 4.5   Obtaining Information About the Characteristics of an External File

Goal

Determine information about the characteristics of several external files in a directory. Write this information and a specific number of data lines from each external file to a report.

Strategy

Write a DATA _NULL_ step to obtain information about the files in a directory and produce a report.

Determine the name of the directory that you want to examine. Assign the name to a SAS variable.

Open the directory with the FILENAME and DOPEN functions. Find the number of files in the directory with the DNUM function. Write an iterative DO loop that iterates the number of times equal to the number of files in the directory.

On each iteration of the DO loop, obtain the name of an external file in the directory with the DREAD function. Open the external file and obtain information about the external file with the FILENAME, FOPEN, and FOPTNUM functions.

Write a DO loop to execute within the main DO loop. Iterate this DO loop the number of times equal to the number returned by the FOPTNUM function. On each iteration, write out the information obtained by the FOPTNAME and FINFO functions.

Write another DO loop to execute within the main DO loop. Read data lines from the currently opened external file with this loop. Iterate this DO loop the number of times equal to the number of data lines you want displayed in your report. Read data lines from the external file with the FREAD and FGET functions.

At the bottom of the iteration of the main DO loop, close the external file with the FCLOSE function.

At the bottom of the DATA step, close the directory with the DCLOSE function.

Example Features

This example can execute under the following operating systems:

❐   directory-based systems (OpenVMS, UNIX, Windows)

❐   mainframe (OS/390).

Other features of this example include

❐   partitioned data sets

❐   SAS functions to obtain information about external files.

External File 1

These are the data lines in the section 1 file.

```
Martinez, Marie   98    87    90    92
Hughes, Henry     88    78    87    86
Mann, Lois        76    75    .     .
Marks, Teri       89    91    .     90
Lin, Tom          99   100    90    98
Wicz, Art         84   100    95    98
Baker, Katie      86    81    79    81
Zelaska, Jenny    94    93    98   100
```

These are the data lines in the section 2 file.

```
Mack, Bill        81    77    80    92
Holt, Kathy       96    98    97    86
Chang, Sam        83    85    90    88
Leigh, Joe        74    71    80    82
Glass, Don        87    .     90    95
Gomez, Sandra     91    93    .     88
Trenton, Barb     90    91    89    91
```

These are the data lines in the section 3 file.

```
Moss, Melinda     94    97    90    95
Stanley, Luis     75    .     81    83
Fields, Rosie     82    85    85    85
Banks, Jon        88    90    84    81
Ramirez, Eduardo  83    .     77    .
Kowal, Mickey     93    97    98   100
Cheer, Nancy     100   100   100   100
Meier, Matt       80    83    88    90
```

The data values are aligned in columns and the layout follows.

Field	Column Range
Name of student	1–16
Quiz 1 grade	20–22
Quiz 2 grade	25–27
Quiz 3 grade	30–32
Quiz 4 grade	35–37

Missing grades are denoted by a period.

The three external files exist in one directory and these are the only files in the directory.

Resulting Report

Output 4.5 Report Generated by DATA _NULL_ Step

```
                         Files in Directory


File Name c:\readdata\testdir\example4_8section1.dat
RECFM V
LRECL 256
First 3 Lines: Martinez, Marie      98    87    90    92
               Hughes, Henry         88    78    87    86
               Mann, Lois            76    75    .     .
============================================================
File Name c:\readdata\testdir\example4_8section2.dat
RECFM V
LRECL 256
First 3 Lines: Mack, Bill            81    77    80    92
               Holt, Kathy           96    98    97    86
               Chang, Sam            83    85    90    88
============================================================
File Name c:\readdata\testdir\example4_8section3.dat
RECFM V
LRECL 256
First 3 Lines: Moss, Melinda         94    97    90    95
               Stanley, Luis         75    .     81    83
               Fields, Rosie         82    85    85    85
============================================================
```

Program

This DATA step determines information about the files in a directory by applying SAS functions. It produces a report that includes information about each file in the directory.

This DATA step executes under SAS for Windows.

```
title "Files in Directory";
data _null_;
```

Define a variable whose length is adequate to hold a data line from the external file.

```
  length fileline $ 50
         ckfilename $ 50;
```

Assign the name of the directory to a SAS variable.

```
  checkdir='c:\readdata\testdir\';
```

Direct the results of the PUT statements to the OUTPUT window.

```
  file print;
```

```
  put /;
```

Define a fileref for the directory.	```rc=filename('mydir',checkdir);```

Stop the DATA step if it is not possible to access the directory.	```if rc ne 0 then do;```
	``` file log;```
	``` put '***Unable to access directory: 'checkdir;```
	``` stop;```
	```end;```

Open the directory.	```dirid=dopen('mydir');```
Determine the number of files in the directory.	```nfiles=dnum(dirid);```
Examine each of the files in the directory.	```do i=1 to nfiles;```
Obtain the name of the external file.	``` ckfilename=dread(dirid,i);```
Define a fileref for the external file.	``` rc=filename('ckfilref',checkdir || ckfilename);```

Stop the DATA step if it is not possible to assign a fileref.	``` if rc ne 0 then do;```
	``` file log;```
	``` put '***Unable to access external file: 'ckfilename;```
	``` stop;```
	``` end;```

Open the external file.	``` fileid=fopen('ckfilref');```
Determine the number of information items that can be obtained about the external file.	``` ninfoitems=foptnum(fileid);```
Evaluate each of the information items.	``` do j=1 to ninfoitems;```
Obtain the name of an information item.	``` infoitem=foptname(fileid,j);```
Obtain the value of the information item.	``` infovalue=finfo(fileid,infoitem);```

Write the name and value of the information item to the report.	``` put infoitem infovalue;```
	``` end;```
	
	``` put 'First 3 Lines: ' @;```

| **Extract the first three data lines from the external file.** | ```
do k=1 to 3;
``` |
| **Place a data line from the external file into the File Data Buffer.** | ```
rc=fread(fileid);
``` |
| **Stop the DATA step if it is not possible to read the external file.** | ```
if rc ne 0 then do;
   file log;
   put '***Unable to read from file: ' ckfilename;
   stop;
end;
``` |
| **Extract the first three data lines from the external file.** | ```
rc=fget(fileid,fileline,50);
if rc=0 then put @16 fileline;
``` |
| **Write a message to the log if unable to extract data from the File Data Buffer.** | ```
else do;
   file log;
   put '***Unable to extract data from: ' ckfilename;
``` |
| **Return output destination to PRINT.** | ```
   file print;
end;
end;
``` |
| **Terminate the report information for one external file with text.** | ```
put 60*'=';
``` |
| **Close the currently opened external file.** | ```
rc=fclose(fileid);
``` |
| **Stop the DATA step if it is not possible to close the external file.** | ```
if rc ne 0 then do;
   file log;
   put '***Unable to close external file: ' ckfilename;
   stop;
end;
end;
``` |
| **Close the directory.** | ```
rc=dclose(dirid);
``` |
| **Write a message to the log if unable to close the currently opened directory.** | ```
if rc ne 0 then do;
   file log;
   put '***Unable to close directory: ' checkdir;
end;
run;
``` |
```

A Closer Look

Understanding External File SAS Functions

A variety of SAS functions manipulate external files and directories. These functions can be part of your DATA steps or they can be used in macro language. The %SYSFUNC and %SYSCALL macro functions execute these SAS functions outside of the DATA step.

Common uses of these functions when coded in a macro program are to conditionally execute subsequent DATA and PROC steps in a program, or to add information to titles and other features of the output.

System-specific Information

Directory-Based Systems

On directory-based systems, write the directory specifications as appropriate for your system.

Mainframe Systems

This example can be adapted to execute on a mainframe system when examining the members of a partitioned data set (PDS).

Modify the CHECKDIR variable to hold the name of your PDS. For example, if the name of your PDS is COLLEGE.ENGLISH.SECT101, the assignment statement for CHECKDIR looks as follows:

```
checkdir='college.english.sect101';
```

Modify the second FILENAME statement to construct the full name of the file. An example follows.

```
rc=filename('ckfilref',checkdir || '(' || trim(ckfilename)
            || ')' );
```

Example 4.7 presents another method of processing the members of a PDS.

Example 4.6 Reading an External File from a Remote System, Creating a Data Set on the Remote System, and Presenting the Data Locally

Goal

Create a SAS data set on a remote system by reading an external file stored on the remote system and present the data in a report run on the local system. The SAS/CONNECT product has been licensed.

Strategy

This example requires SAS/CONNECT. Connect to the remote system, submit a program to the remote system to read the external file, and submit a program on the local system to display the data locally. Specify OPTIONS, FILENAME, and LIBNAME statements with parameters for the SAS/CONNECT session.

Example Features

This example can execute under the following operating systems:

❏ directory-based systems (OpenVMS, UNIX, Windows)

❏ mainframe (OS/390).

Other features of this example include

❏ nonstandard data values

❏ SAS/CONNECT.

External File

The external file is on a remote OS/390 system. Each data line in the external file represents tax revenue information for a township.

This is a view of the file on the mainframe showing both character and hexadecimal representation of the data.

```
----+----1----+----2----+----3----+----4----+----5
Thompson        Washington      &
E8999A994444444E8A8898A99005000000329
386472650000000612895736503C0001093C
West Lake        Washington              j
E8AA4D898444444E8A8898A99007800004090
652303125000000612895736508C0000391C
Shoreview       Washington      q
E8998A88A444444E8A8898A99009300002389
286955956000000612895736518C0001090C
Greenbriars     Lake            q
C988989889A4444D8984444440398000137O8
795552991920000312500000058C0009839C
Bascom          Lake            p       g
C8A899444444444D8984444440291000087B9
21236400000000031250000017C0009730C
Mendota         Lake            %       gn<
D8989A844444444D8984444440076000048B4
455463100000000312500000007C0000475C
Stillwater      Lake                    q
EA899A8A8944444D898444444040000002971
239336135900000312500000001C0000080C
Canalport       Lake                    p
C8989999A444444D898444444001900003938
31513769300000 312500000010C0000273C
```

There are eight data lines in this external file. Each data line is represented in the view on three lines with the first being the character representation of the data line. The second two grayed lines are the hexadecimal values for each character. The topmost line is a guide for identifying column numbers.

The data values are aligned in columns and the layout follows.

Field	Column Range
Township name	1–15
County name	16–25
Number of households	26–29
Tax revenue to date	30–37

The number of households and tax revenue, which are numeric, are stored in packed decimal format. Tax revenue has two decimal places.

Resulting Data Set

Output 4.6 TAXES Data Set

```
                        Tax Revenue to Date

  Obs  township    county      households       taxes        average

   1   Thompson    Washington      3500     $100,392.39       $28.68
   2   West Lake   Washington       788      $43,099.10       $54.69
   3   Shoreview   Washington      1983     $120,398.09       $60.72
   4   Greenbriars Lake           35988     $1938730.98       $53.87
   5   Bascom      Lake           21971     $987,738.09       $44.96
   6   Mendota     Lake             776      $44,879.54       $57.83
   7   Stillwater  Lake             410      $20,987.01       $51.19
   8   Canalport   Lake            1109      $32,973.38       $29.73
```

Program	This program creates a data set on a remote OS/390 system by reading an external file stored on the remote OS/390 system. Once the data set is created, the data are displayed locally in a Windows SAS session.
| **Reference the logon script file that is shipped with SAS. Note that this file may have been modified at your installation by your SAS installation representative.** | ```
filename rlink
'c:\programfiles\sasinstitute\v8\connect\saslink\tcpmvs.scr'
;
``` |
| **Indicate that the remote system is an OS/390 MVS system.** | ```
options remote=mvs
``` |
| **Indicate the communications access method.** | ```
        comamid=tcp;
``` |
| **Connect from your local SAS session to a remote SAS session.** | ```
signon;
``` |
| **Signal the start of the code that should execute on the remote system.** | ```
rsubmit;
  data taxes;
``` |
| **Identify the name of the external file on the remote system.** | ```
    infile 'myid.taxes.janweek1';
``` |
| | ```
    input @1  township $15.
          @16 county $10.
          @26 households pd4.
          @30 taxes pd8.2;
``` |
| **Read the data with informats specific to the remote system, which in this example is the OS/390 system.** Read the two numeric variables with packed decimal informats. (Since this code executes on the OS/390 system and not on the local system, the S370F informats that translate EBCDIC code to ASCII could be used, but are not required.) | ```
    average=taxes/households;
    format taxes average dollar12.2;
  run;
``` |
| **Terminate the submission of statements to the remote system.** | ```
endrsubmit;
``` |
| **Specify LIBNAME statement options unique to SAS/CONNECT.** Define a fileref that points to a directory on the remote system. | ```
libname rmtwork
``` |

Identify the library name on the server that should be associated with the fileref RMTWORK.

```
slibref=work
```

Identify the remote session to which you have previously signed on. Specify that the value of the SERVER= option is the same as the value of the REMOTE= option in the OPTIONS statement.

```
server=mvs;
```

Submit a PROC PRINT step from your local SAS session. List locally the data set TAXES found in the library on the remote system that was identified by the SLIBREF= option in the LIBNAME statement.

```
proc print data=rmtwork.taxes;
   title "Tax Revenue to Date";
run;
```

Disconnect from the remote system.

```
signoff;
```

System-specific Information

The example above shows a connection between Windows and OS/390. When using other operating systems, refer to your SAS/CONNECT documentation for coding requirements for the OPTIONS and LIBNAME statements. In addition, check that your INFILE or FILENAME statements specify the external file correctly. The external file in this example is on the remote system and the naming convention follows that of the remote system.

Example 4.7 OS/390: Reading Data from Specific Members of a Partitioned Data Set

Goal

Read data from specific members of a partitioned data set (PDS).

Strategy

Submit a PROC SOURCE statement to create a list of the names of the members in a PDS. Write this list of member names to an external file.

Write a DATA step that reads the list of members and reads data from specific members. Write the DATA step so that on one iteration of the DATA step SAS reads a member name from the list and then reads the entire contents of the member.

Write an INFILE statement and INPUT statement to read a member name from the list. Evaluate the member name. If it meets specific criteria, execute a DO block to read the member. Within the DO block, write an INFILE statement that includes the FILEVAR= and END= options. Specify as the value of the FILEVAR= option the name of the variable that holds the member name.

Following the second INFILE statement, write a DO UNTIL loop that reads the member. Control execution of the loop by testing the value of the END= variable. Stop the loop when the value of the END= variable indicates that SAS has read the last data line in the member.

Example Features

This example can execute under the following operating systems:

❏ mainframe (OS/390).

The INFILE statement options used in this example are the

❏ END= option

❏ FILEVAR= option.

Other features of this example include

❏ PROC SOURCE

❏ partitioned data sets.

External Files

The PDS,
COLLEGE.ENGLISH.COMP101,
contains four members:
SECTION1, SECTION2,
SECTION3, and TEACHERS.

```
  Menu   Functions   Confirm   Utilities   Help
  ------------------------------------------------------------------------------
  LIBRARY          COLLEGE.ENGLISH.COMP101                Row 00001 of 00006
  Command ===>                                            Scroll ===> PAGE
     Name      Prompt     VV MM   Created      Changed      Size  Init  Mod   ID
  _  SECTION1             01.22  01/08/01  01/11/30 09:17    18    16    0   MYID
  _  SECTION2             01.21  01/08/01  01/11/18 13:23    14    16    0   MYID
  _  SECTION3             01.02  01/08/01  01/11/16 14:31    15    15    0   MYID
  _  TEACHERS             01.01  01/07/01  01/07/31 13:49     7     7    0   MYID
```

The members, SECTION1,
SECTION2, and SECTION3,
contain information about
students in three sections of the
English omposition 101 class.
The TEACHERS member
contains information about the
instructors for the three
sections. The example does not
read the TEACHERS member.

These are the data lines in
SECTION1.

```
Martinez, Marie    98    87    90    92
Hughes, Henry      88    78    87    86
Mann, Lois         76    75    .     .
Marks, Teri        89    91    .     90
Lin, Tom           99   100    90    98
Wicz, Art          84   100    95    98
Baker, Katie       86    81    79    81
Zelaska, Jenny     94    93    98   100
```

These are the data lines in
SECTION2.

```
Mack, Bill         81    77    80    92
Holt, Kathy        96    98    97    86
Chang, Sam         83    85    90    88
Leigh, Joe         74    71    80    82
Glass, Don         87    .     90    95
Gomez, Sandra      91    93    .     88
Trenton, Barb      90    91    89    91
```

These are the data lines in
SECTION3.

```
Moss, Melinda      94    97    90    95
Stanley, Luis      75    .     81    83
Fields, Rosie      82    85    85    85
Banks, Jon         88    90    84    81
Ramirez, Eduardo   83    .     77    .
Kowal, Mickey      93    97    98   100
Cheer, Nancy      100   100   100   100
Meier, Matt        80    83    88    90
```

The data values are aligned in columns and the layout follows.

Missing grades are denoted by a period.

Field	Column Range
Name of student	1–16
Quiz 1 grade	20–22
Quiz 2 grade	25–27
Quiz 3 grade	30–32
Quiz 4 grade	35–37

This is a view of the external file that PROC SOURCE creates.

```
SECTION1
SECTION2
SECTION3
TEACHERS
```

Resulting Data Set

PROC SOURCE left aligns the member names and arranges them in alphabetical order.

Output 4.7 STUDENTS Data Set

```
                    Students in English Comp 101

    Obs    student          quiz1   quiz2   quiz3   quiz4   avgquiz

     1     Martinez, Marie    98      87      90      92      91.8
     2     Hughes, Henry      88      78      87      86      84.8
     3     Mann, Lois         76      75       .       .      75.5
     4     Marks, Teri        89      91       .      90      90.0
     5     Lin, Tom           99     100      90      98      96.8
     6     Wicz, Art          84     100      95      98      94.3
     7     Baker, Katie       86      81      79      81      81.8
     8     Zelaska, Jenny     94      93      98     100      96.3
     9     Mack, Bill         81      77      80      92      82.5
    10     Holt, Kathy        96      98      97      86      94.3
    11     Chang, Sam         83      85      90      88      86.5
    12     Leigh, Joe         74      71      80      82      76.8
    13     Glass, Don         87       .      90      95      90.7
    14     Gomez, Sandra      91      93       .      88      90.7
    15     Trenton, Barb      90      91      89      91      90.3
    16     Moss, Melinda      94      97      90      95      94.0
    17     Stanley, Luis      75       .      81      83      79.7
    18     Fields, Rosie      82      85      85      85      84.3
    19     Banks, Jon         88      90      84      81      85.8
    20     Ramirez, Eduard    83       .      77       .      80.0
    21     Kowal, Mickey      93      97      98     100      97.0
    22     Cheer, Nancy      100     100     100     100     100.0
    23     Meier, Matt        80      83      88      90      85.3
```

Program

This program determines the member names of a PDS and then reads selected members of that PDS into a data set.

This program uses the SOURCE procedure, which is part of base SAS in the OS/390 environment only. PROC SOURCE provides several utility features for processing OS/390 files.

Process a PDS. Suppress printed output generated by PROC SOURCE.

```
proc source noprint
```

Produce a list of member names, but do not read the members.

```
                     nodata
```

Specify either the physical name of the input PDS or a fileref for the input PDS name.

```
                indd='college.english.comp101'
```

Specify either the physical name or the fileref of the destination of the output from PROC SOURCE.

```
                dirdd='myid.comp101.list';
run;
```

Specify the length of the variable that holds the full name of the input member.

```
data students;
  length fullname $ 100;
```

Read the member names from the external file created by PROC SOURCE in the step above.

```
  infile 'myid.comp101.list';
  input fullname $ ;
```

Examine the member name and process only the members that contain SECTION in the name.

```
  if index(upcase(fullname),'SECTION') > 0 then do;
```

Store the complete name of the external file in the variable FULLNAME. Concatenate the member name to the PDS name.

```
    fullname='college.english.comp101(' ||
          trim(fullname) || ')';
```

Specify DUMMY as a placeholder for the required file-specification in the INFILE statement.

```
    infile dummy
```

Read from the member whose name is the current value of FULLNAME.

```
        filevar=fullname
```

Define a variable that SAS sets to 1 when it reads the last data line in the member.

```
        end=endmember;
```

Read each data line from the member whose name is the current value of FULLNAME. Stop the loop when SAS detects that it has read the last data line from the member.

```
   do until(endmember);
      input student $ 1-16 quiz1-quiz4;
```

Compute the average quiz score by using the MEAN function.

```
      avgquiz=mean(of quiz1-quiz4);
```

Write each student record to the STUDENTS data set.

```
      output students;
    end;
  end;
run;
proc print data=students;
  title 'Students in English Comp 101';
  var student quiz1-quiz4 avgquiz;
  format avgquiz 5.1;
run;
```

A Closer Look

Understanding the File That PROC SOURCE Creates with the DIRDD= Option

The DIRDD= option identifies the output destination of the PROC SOURCE procedure. Each data line in the destination contains information about one member of the PDS. Each dataline is 80 bytes in length. SAS left-aligns the PDS member name and pads the name on the right with blanks.

Understanding the Processing of this DATA step

In this example, the number of iterations of the DATA step is equal to the number of data lines in MYID.COMP101.LIST plus one. (On the last iteration, SAS detects no more data lines in MYID.COMP101.LIST and stops the step.) Without the OUTPUT statement in the DO UNTIL loop, SAS would output only the last data line from each of the three section files. The DO UNTIL loop iterates the number of data lines in the external file currently being read.

Where to Go From Here

For specific information on the data stored in the directory records generated by PROC SOURCE, refer to IBM OS/390 documentation.

Example 4.8 OS/390: Reading a VSAM KSDS Data Set

Goal

Read specific records identified by keys from a VSAM KSDS data set stored on an OS/390 computer. Read the VSAM KSDS data set with keyed direct access.

Strategy

Determine the keys that should be read from the VSAM KSDS data set. In this example, read the keys from the external file in which they were stored.

Write the DATA step so that in one iteration the step first reads one key from the list of keys and then second searches the VSAM KSDS data set for the record with that key.

Specify an INFILE statement and an INPUT statement to read a key from the list of keys.

Specify a second INFILE statement that identifies the VSAM KSDS data set. Add the VSAM option to this INFILE statement to indicate that you are processing a VSAM data set.

Specify the KEY= option in the second INFILE statement to indicate that you want to find a record in the VSAM KSDS data set with keyed direct access. Set as the value of the KEY= option the name of the variable that holds the key value.

Define with the FEEDBACK= option in the second INFILE statement a variable that can be tested to determine the success of the keyed direct access read of the VSAM data set.

Test whether the record identified by the KEY= variable's value can be found by writing an INPUT statement that reads no variables. Include in this statement a trailing @ to keep the data line in the input buffer for further processing later in the DATA step.

Test the value of the FEEDBACK= variable to determine the success of the keyed direct access lookup. For lookups that succeed, write an INPUT statement to read the VSAM record.

For lookups that indicate that the record was not found, reset the _ERROR_ and FEEDBACK= variables to 0 so that the DATA step continues processing. Include this key in the output data set and assign informative text to one of the variables so that the results can easily be identified when viewing the resulting data set.

For all other non-zero return codes, write an error message to the SAS log and stop the program.

Example Features

This example can execute under the following operating systems:

❑ mainframe (OS/390).

The INFILE statement options used in this example are the

❑ FEEDBACK= option

❑ KEY= option

❑ VSAM option.

The INPUT statement feature used in this example is the

❑ trailing @.

Other features of this example include:

❑ VSAM data set processing.

External File 1

This first external file contains the five keys to find in the VSAM file.

```
AB8372583U
II3757293Z
JY0937639Q
RA3863296P
CV7338728E
```

The key is the driver's license id and it is 10 characters wide. Assume that the second key in the list is not in the VSAM KSDS data set.

External File 2

This view of the second external file is a snapshot of the VSAM data set. Assume the VSAM data set contains millions of records.

```
AB8372583USMITH           JOSEPH          A05151970
AZ8372962OEVANS           MARGARET         11231959
BJ3769273YLEE             LINDA           L04021965
CV7338728ECARLSON         JOANNE          Z03281968
CZ3872764AANDERSON        JAMES           T08141952
GE6737863PRICH            ROBERT          W10201963
HU1937638VLOUIS           KATRINKA        A01151982
JY0937639QRAMIREZ         ROSA            D12011954
RA3863296PBOLDT           BRUCE           M09301962
```

The data values are aligned in columns and the layout follows.

Field	Column Range
Driver's license ID	1–10
Last name	11–28
First name	29–43
Middle initial	44
Date of birth	45–54

Resulting Data Set

***Output 4.8 FINDDRIVER
Data Set***

```
                  Results of VSAM Key Lookup

Obs     dlid      lastname      firstname    mi        dob

 1   AB8372583U   SMITH          JOSEPH      A    05/15/1970
 2   II3757293Z   ** NOT FOUND                            .
 3   JY0937639Q   RAMIREZ        ROSA        D    12/01/1954
 4   RA3863296P   BOLDT          BRUCE       M    09/30/1962
 5   CV7338728E   CARLSON        JOANNE      Z    03/28/1968
```

Program

This DATA step searches a VSAM KSDS data set for records with specific keys. It uses keyed direct access to find the records.

```
data finddriver;
   infile 'myid.finddriv.dat';
```

Identify the external file that contains the keys that should be searched for in the VSAM KSDS data set.

Read each key with formatted input.

```
   input dlid $10.;
```

Identify the VSAM KSDS file.

```
   infile 'minnesota.drivers.ksds'
```

Indicate that this is a VSAM file.

```
          vsam
```

Specify the variable that identifies the keys that the program should find.

```
          key=dlid
```

Define a variable that holds the return code that results from the search for the key.

```
          feedback=vsamrc;
```

Attempt to find the record in the VSAM KSDS with an INPUT statement, but do not read in any variables. Keep a "found" record in the input buffer with the trailing @ so that a later INPUT statement can read data from the VSAM record.

```
   input @;
```

Test the value of the return code produced by the INPUT @ statement and stored in the FEEDBACK= variable. For records not found, which is indicated by a return code of 16, process this DO block.

```
if vsamrc=16 then do;
```

Reset the _ERROR_ automatic variable to 0 so that processing continues and so that SAS does not write any messages to the SAS log.

```
   _error_=0;
```

Assign text to the value of LASTNAME so that records not found can be easily identified in the PROC PRINT report.

```
   lastname='** Not Found';
```

Include this record in the data set.

```
   output;
```

Prevent execution of the remaining statements in the DATA step and return to the top of the step.

```
   return;
end;
```

Stop processing the DATA step for all other nonzero return codes.

```
else if vsamrc ne 0 then do;
   put '**** Unknown Error, Program Halted ' vsamrc=;
   stop;
end;
```

For records found, read the VSAM record with formatted input.

```
input @11 lastname $18. firstname $15. mi $1.
         dob mmddyy8.;
```

Write this observation to the output data set.

```
   output;
   format dob mmddyy10.;
run;
proc print data=finddriver;
   title 'Results of VSAM Key Lookup';
run;
```

Where to Go From Here

This example shows only one of several types of VSAM data sets. For detailed information on processing VSAM data sets, refer to *SAS Guide to VSAM Processing*.

Example 4.9 Directory-based Systems: Reading a Fixed-Length EBCDIC File on an ASCII System

Goal

Read an external file that was downloaded in binary mode from a mainframe to an ASCII system. Some of the data values in the external file are stored as nonstandard data. The external file on the mainframe is fixed in length.

Strategy

Transfer the external file from the mainframe in binary mode so that the EBCDIC encoding of the data is preserved. Determine the record length of the external file that you are downloading from the mainframe so that you can include this information in the INFILE statement that reads the downloaded file.

After downloading the external file, write and execute a DATA step to read the external file. Specify the record format and logical record length of the ASCII system file in the INFILE statement. Indicate that the external file is fixed in length with RECFM=F. Specify the logical record length with the LRECL= option.

On the INPUT statement that reads the downloaded external file, associate S370F type informats and the $EBCDIC*w*. informat to the variables.

Example Features

This example can execute under the following operating systems:

❐ directory-based systems (OpenVMS, UNIX, Windows).

The INFILE statement options used in this example are the

❐ LRECL= option

❐ RECFM= option.

Other features of this example include

❐ nonstandard data values.

External File

The external file contains information about packages received. This is a view of the file on the mainframe showing both character and hexadecimal representation of the data.

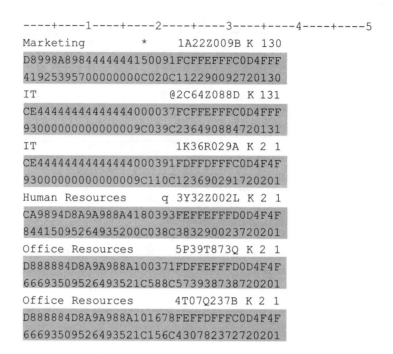

```
----+----1----+----2----+----3----+----4----+----5
Marketing        *     1A22Z009B K 130
D8998A8984444444150091FCFFEFFFC0D4FFF
41925395700000000C020C112290092720130
IT                     @2C64Z088D K 131
CE4444444444444444000037FCFFEFFFC0D4FFF
93000000000000000009C039C236490884720131
IT                     1K36R029A K 2 1
CE4444444444444444000391FDFFDFFFC0D4F4F
93000000000000000009C110C123690291720201
Human Resources    q 3Y32Z002L K 2 1
CA9894D8A9A988A4180393FEFFEFFFD0D4F4F
8441509526493520000C038C383290023720201
Office Resources       5P39T873Q K 2 1
D888884D8A9A988A100371FDFFEFFFD0D4F4F
66693509526493521C588C573938738720201
Office Resources       4T07Q237B K 2 1
D888884D8A9A988A101678FEFFDFFFC0D4F4F
66693509526493521C156C430782372720201
```

The file contains six data lines. Each data line is represented in the view in three lines with the first being the character representation of the data line. The second two grayed lines are the hexadecimal values for each character. The topmost line is a guide for identifying column numbers.

The data values are aligned in columns and the layout follows.

Variable	Type	Column Range	Storage Format
Department	Character	1–16	Character
Department ID	Numeric	17–18	Packed decimal
Cost	Numeric	19–22	Packed decimal, with 2 decimal places
Package ID	Character	23–31	Character
Shipment date Year	Numeric	32–33	Positive integer binary
Shipment date month	Numeric	34–35	Standard numeric
Shipment date day	Numeric	36–37	Standard numreic

The attributes of the external file on the Mainframe are

❐ fixed block record format

❐ logical record length=37

❐ blocksize=22496.

The attributes of the external file that is downloaded from the mainframe to the ASCII system are

❏ fixed record format

❏ logical record length=37.

This is the view of the external file on the ASCII system.

```
Ô ™′…£‰•‡@@@@@@@Ł\`ˆ  ñÁòòéõõùÂ¨Ò´-Éã@@@@@@@@@@@@@@@
`˜9|òÃõõéõøøÄ¨Ò´Éã@@@@@@@@@@@@@@@
´1  ñÒóõÙõòùÁ¨Ò^´È¤″ •@Ù…¢-
¤™ƒ…¢@ŁŒ`3˜<óèóòéõõòó¨Ò^´Ö††‰ƒ…@Ù…¢-¤™ƒ…¢ł
˜8x õ×óùãø÷óØ¨Ò^´Ö††‰ƒ…@Ù…¢-¤™ƒ…¢ł
łevŒôãõ÷øòó÷Â¨Ò^´
```

An EBCDIC file transferred to an ASCII system as a binary stream looks like a series of unreadable characters. Here the data is shown over several lines. When viewed with a text editor, the data for this example look like they are all on one line.

Resulting Data Set

Output 4.9 PROC PRINT of SHIPINFO Data Set

```
              Recent Shipment Information

Obs  dept            deptid     cost   packageid    shipdate

 1   Marketing          105   $29.01   1A22Z009B   01/30/2002
 2   IT                  90   $33.97   2C64Z088D   01/31/2002
 3   IT                  90  $1,319.01 1K36R029A   02/01/2002
 4   Human Resources    108  $339.83   3Y32Z002L   02/01/2002
 5   Office Resources   110  $5,387.81 5P39T873Q   02/01/2002
 6   Office Resources   110  $11657.68 4T07Q237B   02/01/2002
```

Program

This DATA step reads an external file stored on an ASCII system. The file was downloaded in binary mode from an EBCDIC system. In this example, the external file was transferred from a mainframe to a Windows system.

Specify the name of the external file that was transferred from the mainframe to Windows.

```
data shipinfo;
   infile 'c:\readdata\example4_9.dat'
```

Specify the attributes of the external file.

```
                     recfm=f lrecl=37;
```

Specify the S370F informats to translate EBCDIC nonstandard data to ASCII.
Translate EBCDIC character data to ASCII character data with the $EBCDICw. informat.

```
   input dept        $ebcdic16.
```

Translate EBCDIC packed decimal data to ASCII numeric data with the S370FPD informat.

```
         deptid    s370fpd2.
         cost      s370fpd4.2
         packageid $ebcdic9.
```

Translate EBCDIC positive integer binary data to ASCII numeric data with the S370FPIB informat.

```
         shipyear   s370fpib2.
```

Translate EBCDIC numeric data to ASCII numeric data with the S370FF informat.

```
         shipmonth s370ff2.
         shipday   s370ff2.;

   drop shipyear shipmonth shipday;
```

Create SHIPDATE as a SAS date by applying the MDY function to the shipping month, day, and year.

```
   shipdate=mdy(shipmonth,shipday,shipyear);
   format cost dollar9.2 shipdate mmddyy10.;
run;
proc print data=shipinfo;
   title "Recent Shipment Information";
run;
```

A Closer Look

Comparing the EBCDIC Encoding System to the ASCII Encoding System

Mainframes encode data in the EBCDIC character encoding system. Operating systems such as Windows, UNIX, and OpenVMS encode data in ASCII. Data values are represented differently internally in the two systems. File structures can also be different on the two systems.

As long as you work with your EBCDIC file on an EBCDIC system and your ASCII file on an ASCII system, you will not have to take the character encoding system into consideration. When you work between systems and you want to read or write raw data, you may have to use special informats and formats that SAS provides to work with data stored in a different encoding system.

Moving an External File from an EBCDIC System to an ASCII System

The external file in this example is downloaded using an FTP (File Transfer Protocol) program. FTP programs usually default to converting EBCDIC data to ASCII when transferring a file from a mainframe to a PC.

When your external file contains only standard numeric and character data, the FTP program will correctly convert the EBCDIC data to ASCII.

When your external file contains nonstandard numeric or character data, the FTP program will not correctly convert the EBCDIC data to ASCII. The FTP program examines each byte and sometimes a byte in a nonstandard numeric field will look like a standard character to the FTP program. In those situations, the FTP program will change the byte to the corresponding ASCII character. As a result, the contents of the downloaded external file are no longer correct.

Understanding File Structures

File structures differ on mainframes and ASCII systems.

Mainframe files are either fixed or variable in structure with information about the attributes of the file stored with the file. When a file has variable-length records, information about each record is stored with each record as well.

Files on ASCII systems do not store information about the attributes of the file within the file. Instead, ASCII files have an End-of-Record (EOR) marker at the end of each record to flag the end of the record.

The EOR marker can vary between different ASCII systems. Under Windows, the EOR is a carriage return and line feed. On UNIX, the EOR is just the line feed.

An external file downloaded from an EBCDIC system as a fixed-length file will not contain EOR markers. Therefore, when working with fixed-length EBCDIC files, it is important to specify the record length exactly in the INFILE statement that reads the downloaded file.

When you download a variable-length EBCDIC file with an FTP program, the FTP program will evaluate each record and place an EOR marker at the end of each record. If your variable length external file contains only standard character and numeric data, the transfer with translation from EBCDIC to ASCII and insertion of EOR markers will not cause problems in reading the data with SAS. If your variable-length file contains nonstandard numeric or character data, however, and you download it in binary mode, SAS cannot correctly read the external file because the FTP program removes information SAS needs to determine record length.

A way to read variable-length files that contain nonstandard numeric or character data is with the FTP access method. This allows you to read the external file from the mainframe without downloading it. Chapter 6 contains examples of using the FTP access method. Additional ways of processing variable-length files that contain nonstandard numeric or character data are beyond the scope of this book. See "Where to Go From Here" for references.

Using the S370F Informats and Formats

When working with nonstandard data, such as packed decimal and integer binary, you may want to use the S370F type informats and formats to read and write the data values. This enables you to run the same program on systems that use different byte storage systems. Using the S370F type informats and formats can prevent errors when sharing data and programs between IBM mainframes and ASCII systems.

To read character data written in EBCDIC from an ASCII system, use the SAS $EBCDICw.$ informat.

Transferring Files Between Systems with SAS/CONNECT

An external file can be transferred using an FTP program available on the system you are using. If you have SAS/CONNECT, you can also transfer a file using PROC DOWNLOAD.

To transfer a file using SAS/CONNECT, sign on to the remote system from your local SAS session. For example, you can submit the following commands from a Windows session to connect to an OS/390 system.

Define a fileref to the logon script file that is shipped with SAS.

```
filename rlink
'c:\programfiles\sasinstitute\v8\connect\saslink\tcpmvs.scr';
```

Identify that the remote system is an OS/390 MVS system.

```
options remote=mvs
```

Specify the communications access method.

```
        comamid=tcp;
```

Connect from the local SAS session to a remote SAS session on the OS/390 system.

```
signon;
```

Name the external file that the download will create.

```
filename local 'c:\readdata\example4_9.dat';
```

Signal the start of the code that should execute on the remote system.

```
rsubmit;
```

Identify the remote file. When transferring a file as a binary stream to a Windows system, specify the file to download as RECFM=U and BLKSIZE=32760.

```
filename remote 'myid.packages.dat' recfm=u blksize=32760;
```

Identify the input and output files.

Override the default method of transferring a file as a text file. Tranferring the file as a binary file preserves the EBCDIC coding of the file when it is written to the local system.

```
proc download infile=remote
                outfile=local
                binary;
run;
```

Terminate the submission of statements to the remote system.

```
endsubmit;
```

Disconnect from the remote system.

```
signoff;
```

Related Technique

The FTP access method allows you to read an external file stored on a remote host system without downloading the external file. This method can read either fixed- or variable-length files that contain standard or nonstandard data values. See the FTP access method examples in Chapter 6.

Where to Go From Here

The technical support document TS-642 "Reading EBCDIC Files on ASCII Systems" explains in detail the differences between the EBCDIC and ASCII systems. It addresses reading EBCDIC files on ASCII systems.

For complete documentation on the S370 type informats and formats, refer to *SAS Language Reference: Dictionary*.

Consult *SAS/CONNECT User's Guide* for complete documentation on using SAS/CONNECT.

Example 4.10 Reading Variable-Length Data Lines from a Binary Stream File

Goal

Read a binary stream file where the data lines are variable in length and some of the data values vary in width. Specify the widths that vary in the input data line.

Strategy

Direct that the file be read as a binary stream by specifying the RECFM=N option in the INFILE statement. Include the double trailing @ (@@) in the INPUT statements to keep the binary stream data line in the input buffer during all iterations of the DATA step.

Add the EOF= option to the INFILE statement. Specify as the value of the EOF= option a statement label that SAS directs processing to when it detects the end of the external file. At the end of the DATA step, specify the label named with the EOF= option. Separate the statements preceding the statement label from the statement label with a RETURN statement.

Place a STOP statement after the statement label to release the input data line from the input buffer and stop the DATA step.

Read the width of the varying width data values from the input data lines. Use these values with the $VARYINGw. informat to read the varying width data values.

Example Features

This example can execute under the following operating systems:

❏ directory-based systems (UNIX, Windows). Note that RECFM=N is not available under OpenVMS.

❏ mainframe (OS/390) when the OS/390 file has a RECFM of F (fixed), FS (fixed spanned), or FBS (fixed block spanned).

The INFILE statement options used in this example are the

❏ EOF= option

❏ RECFM= option.

The INPUT statement features used in this example are the

❏ double trailing @ (@@)

❏ $VARYING informat.

External File

The external file contains
information about attendance
at selected activities.

```
Y7Johnson422Field Trip and BanquetY5Adams222Field Trip
and BanquetN8JacobsonY9Stevenson213WorkshopOnlyY6Walker
420Banquet and WorkshopN8MorrisonY5Green314All
ActivitiesN3Lee
```

When viewed with a text editor, the external file looks like one long
data line. To completely display the data line on this page, the data line
is wrapped.

This long data line contains data values for eight observations. The
data values for an observation are found in the following order. There
are no delimiters between the data values.

❐   attendance at the event (Y/N): width of 1

❐   length of the field that contains the family's last name

❐   family's last name

The next three fields are only included when attendance at the event is **Y**.

❐   the number of people attending: width of 1

❐   the length of the activity text

❐   the activity text

Observations where attendance at the event is **N** do not have any data
values recorded for these three fields nor do they have missing value
placeholders.

Resulting Data Set

Output 4.10 PROC PRINT of
ATTENDANCE Data Set

```
                  Families by Attendance

--------------------- attend=N ---------------------

       Obs      family      howmany      activity

        1       Jacobson       0           None
        2       Lee            0           None
        3       Morrison       0           None


--------------------- attend=Y ---------------------

      Obs      family     howmany      activity

       4       Adams        2        Field Trip and Banquet
       5       Green        3        All Activities
       6       Johnson      4        Field Trip and Banquet
       7       Stevenson    2        Workshop Only
       8       Walker       4        Banquet and Workshop
```

Program

This DATA step reads an external file where the data values are stored in a binary stream. Some of the fields vary in width and the widths of these fields are included in the input data line.

```
data attendance;
   infile 'c:\readdata\example4_10.dat'
          recfm=n
```

Specify that the external file consists of a stream of bytes with no record boundaries.

Direct processing to the label LAST when SAS reaches the end of the external file and thus prevent the DATA step from executing indefinitely.

```
          eof=last;
```

Drop these two variables since they are not needed in the output data set.

```
   drop famlength actlength;

   input attend $1.
         famlength 1.
```

Read the length of the FAMILY variable.

Set the length of the FAMILY variable to 9. Follow the $VARYING informat with the name of the variable that contains the width of the current value of the FAMILY variable.

```
         family $varying9. famlength
```

Keep the one and only data line in the input buffer for subsequent iterations of the DATA step and thus prevent termination of the DATA step before SAS reads all the observations.

```
   @@;
```

Read additional data about families that are attending.

```
   if attend='Y' then do;
      input howmany 1.
            actlength 2.
```

Read the width of the current value of the ACTIVITY variable, which like FAMILY varies in width.

Set the length of the ACTIVITY variable to 22. Follow the $VARYING informat with the name of the variable that contains the width of the current value of the ACTIVITY variable.

```
            activity $varying22. actlength
```

Keep the data line in the input buffer for subsequent iterations of the DATA step and thus prevent termination of the DATA step before SAS reads all the observations.	``` @@; end; ```
Set default values to the variables HOWMANY and ACTIVITY for families not attending.	``` else if attend='N' then do; howmany=0; activity='None'; end; ```
Return to the top of the DATA step to read the next observation.	``` return; ```
Execute this section when SAS reaches the end of the external file.	``` last: ```
Write a message to the SAS log.	``` put 'Reached end of file'; ```
Stop the program before this last iteration of the DATA step completely executes and prevent SAS from outputting an observation with all missing data.	``` stop; run; ```

```
proc sort data=attendance;
  by attend family;
run;
proc print data=attendance;
  title "Families by Attendance";
  by attend;
  var family howmany activity;
run;
```

Example 4.11 Directory-based Systems: Reading Multiple External Files from a Directory

Goal

Read multiple external files from a directory. Produce a list of the files to read by issuing a system command. Use this list to determine the files to read.

Strategy

Create an unnamed pipe by specifying the PIPE option in the FILENAME statement. Include in this FILENAME statement the system command that produces the list of external files to read.

Write one DATA step that reads from the list the names of the files that should be read and that also reads the contents of each file on the list. In one iteration of the DATA step, read a name from the list of filenames and completely read that external file.

In the first INFILE statement reference the fileref of the pipe. Follow this with an INPUT statement that reads the list of filenames. Under most operating systems, add the full path of the filename to the beginning of the variable that holds the filename. Ensure that an ATTRIB or LENGTH statement defines this variable with a width adequate to contain the full name of the external file.

In the second INFILE statement, specify the FILEVAR= option with the name of the variable defined in the first INPUT statement. Specify a fileref in this INFILE statement that serves only as a placeholder. This fileref can be any text string not already defined as a fileref.

Also in the second INFILE statement, add the END= option to define a variable that SAS sets to **1** when it reads the last data line in the external file. Follow the INPUT statement with a DO UNTIL loop that reads the external file. Control execution of the loop by testing the value of the END= variable. Stop the loop when the value of the END= variable indicates that SAS has read the last data line in the external file.

Example Features

This example can execute under the following operating systems:

❒ directory-based systems (OpenVMS, UNIX, Windows).

The INFILE statement options used in this example are the

❒ END= option

❒ FILEVAR= option

❒ TRUNCOVER option.

Other features of this example include

❒ FILENAME statement specifications.

External Files

The three external files contain data about pollen counts for the first seven days of September. Each external file contains evaluations for a specific location: campus, park, or suburb.

These are the campus data lines. The filename is pollencampus.dat.

```
09/01/2002 Medium     Grass
09/02/2002 Low        Mold spores
09/03/2002 High       Grass, Ragweed
09/04/2002 Medium     Grass
09/05/2002 Medium     Grass, Mold spores
09/06/2002 Extreme    Ragweed
09/07/2002 Extreme    Ragweed
```

These are the park data lines. The filename is pollenpark.dat.

```
09/01/2002 High       Ragweed, Grass
09/02/2002 Extreme    Mold spores
09/03/2002 High       Mold spores, Ragweed, Grass
09/04/2002 Extreme    Ragweed
09/05/2002 Medium     Grass
09/06/2002 Medium     Grass
09/07/2002 Medium     Grass
```

These are the suburb data lines. The filename is pollensuburb.dat.

```
09/01/2002 Negligible Mold spores
09/02/2002 Low        Mold spores
09/03/2002 Low        Mold spores
09/04/2002 Medium     Mold spores, Ragweed
09/05/2002 High       Ragweed, Grass
09/06/2002 High       Ragweed, Grass
09/07/2002 High       Ragweed, Grass
```

The data values are aligned in columns and the layout follows.

Field	Column Range
Date of the pollen count (mm/dd/yyyy)	1–10
Level of pollen	12–21
Predominant sources of pollen for that day	23–52

Resulting Data Set

Output 4.11 PROC PRINT of POLLEN Data Set

```
                    Pollen Count by Location and Date

Obs  location  pollendate   level       sourcetext

  1   Campus   09/01/2002   Medium      Grass
  2   Campus   09/02/2002   Low         Mold spores
  3   Campus   09/03/2002   High        Grass, Ragweed
  4   Campus   09/04/2002   Medium      Grass
  5   Campus   09/05/2002   Medium      Grass, Mold spores
  6   Campus   09/06/2002   Extreme     Ragweed
  7   Campus   09/07/2002   Extreme     Ragweed
  8   Park     09/01/2002   High        Ragweed, Grass
  9   Park     09/02/2002   Extreme     Mold spores
 10   Park     09/03/2002   High        Mold spores, Ragweed, Grass
 11   Park     09/04/2002   Extreme     Ragweed
 12   Park     09/05/2002   Medium      Grass
 13   Park     09/06/2002   Medium      Grass
 14   Park     09/07/2002   Medium      Grass
 15   Suburb   09/01/2002   Negligible  Mold spores
 16   Suburb   09/02/2002   Low         Mold spores
 17   Suburb   09/03/2002   Low         Mold spores
 18   Suburb   09/04/2002   Medium      Mold spores, Ragweed
 19   Suburb   09/05/2002   High        Ragweed, Grass
 20   Suburb   09/06/2002   High        Ragweed, Grass
 21   Suburb   09/07/2002   High        Ragweed, Grass
```

Program

This DATA step reads data from several external files. A system command generates a list of the files to read and this list is passed to the DATA step through an unnamed pipe. This example executes under Windows.

Specify the PIPE option in the FILENAME statement so that the results of the system command are associated with the fileref.

```
filename filelist pipe
```

Since this program runs under Windows, generate a list of filenames with the DOS DIR command. Restrict the DIR command to search a specific directory for files that start with the word "pollen" and have a file extension of DAT. Include the switch /b in the DIR command, which stands for "bare" and tells DOS that the list should contain just filenames.

```
     'dir c:\readdata\pollen*.dat/b';
data pollen;
```

Define POLLENFILENAME to be 60 bytes to hold the complete name, including the path, of the external file.	`length pollenfilename $ 60 location $ 6;` `format pollendate mmddyy10.;`
Drop these two variables since they are only needed for the duration of the DATA step.	`drop startloc endloc;`
Read from the list of file names generated by the system command specified in the FILENAME statement. Reference the fileref for the pipe in this statement.	`infile filelist`
Prevent the INPUT statement from moving to the next data line if the current data line is not as wide as the INPUT statement expects.	`        truncover;` `input pollenfilename $60.;`
Use STARTLOC and ENDLOC to find the location text in the external file name.	`startloc=index(upcase(pollenfilename),'POLLEN')+6;` `endloc=index(upcase(pollenfilename),'.DAT');`
Extract the text of the location from the value of POLLENFILENAME and place this in the variable LOCATION.	`location=substr(pollenfilename,startloc,endloc-startloc);`
Fully define the external filename by concatentaing the path and the filename.	`pollenfilename='c:\books\readdata\' ||` `                trim(pollenfilename);`
Specify DUMMY as a fileref to serve solely as a placeholder for the file-specification.	`infile dummy`
Read data from the file specified by the current value of the variable POLLENFILENAME.	`        filevar=pollenfilename`
Prevent the INPUT statement from moving to the next data line if the current data line is not as wide as the INPUT statement expects.	`        truncover`
Define a variable that SAS sets to 1 when it reads the last data line in the external file.	`        end=lastrec;`

191

Execute this DO UNTIL loop for every data line in the file identified by the current value of POLLENFILENAME. Stop the loop when SAS sets LASTREC to **1** because it read the last data line in the currently opened file.

```
  do until (lastrec);
```

Read these external files with formatted input.

```
    input @1  pollendate mmddyy10.
          @12 level $10.
          @23 sourcetext $30.;
```

Include an OUTPUT statement in this DO UNTIL block so that SAS writes every observation to the output data set.

```
     output;
   end;
run;
proc print data=pollen;
  title "Pollen Count by Location and Date";
run;
```

🔍 **A Closer Look**

Understanding How This DATA Step Executes

This DATA step iterates once for each file in the list created by the DIR command. SAS first reads a filename from the list. The second INFILE and INPUT statements then read all the data lines from that file.

The DO UNTIL loop controls the reading of each external file. SAS sets the value of LASTREC to **1** when it reads the last data line in the file currently opened. For files after the first, SAS resets the value of LASTREC to **0** when the second INFILE statement executes on subsequent iterations.

The OUTPUT statement must be included so that every data line in the external file is written to the output data set. By default, when an OUTPUT statement is not present in a DATA step, SAS writes an observation to a DATA set only at the bottom of the DATA step, at the end of an iteration of the DATA step. In this example, if the OUTPUT statement was omitted, data set POLLEN would contain only the three observations created from the last data line in each of the three external files.

System-specific Information

Operating systems other than mainframe operating systems, Windows 3.1, and DOS support the PIPE option in the FILENAME statement. All follow the same syntax:

```
FILENAME fileref  PIPE 'system command';
```

UNIX pipes

An example of a FILENAME statement written for a UNIX system follows.

```
filename filelist pipe
          'ls -1 /readdata/pollen*';
```

This FILENAME statement that includes character matching of the filenames generates a list of filenames that includes the path. Therefore, the statement in the DATA step that adds the path to the filename would not be included.

If the character matching part of the command was omitted, UNIX would generate a list of filenames that excludes the path. In this situation, you would keep the assignment statement in the DATA step that adds the path to the filename.

When in doubt, always test the system command first to view the type of information that it generates so that you can appropriately write your INPUT statements and assignment statements.

Where to Go From Here

Your host-specific SAS Companion documentation provides more detailed information in specifying unnamed pipes and system commands.

Refer to the technical support document, TS-581 "Using FILEVAR= to Read Multiple External Files in a DATA Step" for more information on applying the FILEVAR= option.

Example 4.12 Reading an External File That Contains Carriage-Control Characters in the First Byte

Goal

Read an external file that contains carriage-control characters in the first byte. Do not retain the carriage-control information in the data set.

Strategy

Specify the PRINT option in the INFILE statement so that SAS ignores carriage-control characters in the first byte of the external file. Include the TRUNCOVER option in the INFILE statement so that SAS does not move to the next data line if the current data line is not as wide as the INPUT statement expects.

Add processing statements to the DATA step to skip over specific data lines based on the content of the data line. Read each data line with two INPUT statements. In the first INPUT statement, add a trailing at sign (@) to keep the data line in the input buffer. Read the part of the data line that will determine whether the data line should be processed any further.

If the data line should be processed, then read additional data from the data line, this time reading the remainder of the variables from the data line. Otherwise, reject the data line and return to the top of the DATA step.

Example Features

This example can execute under the following operating systems:

❐ directory-based systems (OpenVMS, UNIX, Windows)

❐ mainframe (OS/390).

The INFILE statement options used in this example are the

❐ PRINT option

❐ TRUNCOVER option.

The INPUT statement feature used in this example is the

❐ trailing @.

Example Features

This external file contains heights, weights, and body mass indices for 12 subjects from two different study groups.

```
□              Results for Study Group A

  A     101      120        65        19.9654
  A     102      183        70        26.2530
  A     105      189        68        28.7322
  A     108      178        74        22.8497
  A     110      176        70        25.2488
  A     111      132        67        20.6704
□              Results for Study Group B

  B     103      155
  B     104      101        62        18.4698
  B     106      193        68        29.3403
  B     107      210        72        28.4760
  B     109      168        66        27.1110
  B     112      125        63        22.1388
```

Assume this external file is a report generated by a program. This report has two pages with a title on each page and a blank line separating the title and the first line of data.

The external file has carriage-control characters in the first byte. The symbol, □, represents the character that tells the printer to issue a page eject. This external file represents two pages of a report.

The data lines other than the titles or blank lines contain information about the subjects. Each of these lines represents data recorded for one subject. The columns in those lines in order are

1. subject's group

2. subject's id

3. subject's weight in pounds

4. subject's height in inches

5. subject's body mass index.

The height and bmi are missing for id 103.

Resulting Data Set

Output 4.12 PROC PRINT of BMI Data Set

```
              Body Mass Index as Read from Report

     Obs      group      id     weight     height      bmi

      1         A        101     120        65       19.9654
      2         A        102     183        70       26.2530
      3         A        105     189        68       28.7322
      4         A        108     178        74       22.8497
      5         A        110     176        70       25.2488
      6         A        111     132        67       20.6704
      7         B        103     155         .          .
      8         B        104     101        62       18.4698
      9         B        106     193        68       29.3403
     10         B        107     210        72       28.4760
     11         B        109     168        66       27.1110
     12         B        112     125        63       22.1388
```

Program

This DATA step reads an external file that contains carriage-control characters in the first byte. This example runs under Windows where the page eject character is represented by the hexadecimal 12.

```
data bmi;
  infile 'c:\readdata\example4_12.dat'
         print

         truncover;
```

Ignore data in the first byte of every data line.

Prevent the INPUT statement from moving to the next data line if the current data line is not as wide as the INPUT statement expects.

```
length group $ 1;
```

Define a length for the variable that is used to determine the record type.

```
input group $ @;
```

Read GROUP with list input. Keep the data line in the input buffer with the trailing @.

```
if group not in ('A' 'B') then delete;
```

Reject data lines from the report that do not contain subject data.

```
  input id weight height bmi;
run;
proc print data=bmi;
  title 'Body Mass Index as Read from Report';
run;
```

Read subject data lines with list input.

System-Specific Information

The INFILE statement PRINT option is valid under Windows, UNIX, OpenVMS, and OS/390. The default is NOPRINT. The option NOPRINT tells SAS to read carriage-control characters as data values.

Related Technique

Using the FILECC Option Under OpenVMS and OS/390

Under OpenVMS and OS/390, the SAS option FILECC/NOFILECC affects how SAS processes external files that contain carriage-control information. When set to FILECC, this option specifies that data in column one of an external file should be treated as carriage-control information. When set to NOFILECC, SAS treats data in column one as data values.

The FILECC/NOFILECC option can be set several ways:

❏ in the configuration file

❏ at SAS invocation

❏ with the OPTIONS statement

❏ with the OPTIONS window.

The value of the option is in effect throughout the SAS session unless changed with the OPTIONS statement or window during the SAS session. You can also temporarily override the action of the FILECC/NOFILECC option in a DATA step by appropriately specifying the PRINT/NOPRINT option in the INFILE statement that reads the external file.

Example 4.13   OS/390: Reading an External File Created by a COBOL Program

Goal

Read an external file created by a COBOL program.

Strategy

Determine the SAS informats to read the variables by reviewing the way the COBOL program wrote the data values to the external file. Write the DATA step to read the external file fields with the appropriate informats.

Example Features

This example can execute under the following operating systems:

❐   mainframe (OS/390).

Other features of this example include:

❐   nonstandard data values.

External File

This external file contains five data lines with information about budget and costs for five departments.

This is a view of the file on the mainframe showing both character and hexadecimal representation of the data.

```
----+----1----+----2----+----3----+----4----+----5
Accounting0304{   0   b   `       b
C889A9A898FFFFC004F0581037802130282
13364539570304002900520C079C090C122C
Shipping  0314{   0   <   b   <   -@
E889989844FFFFC004F0554048903140267
28977957000314002900390C032C008C170C
Marketing 0321{       q   l       *   *
D8998A8984FFFFC004405920988023507l5
41925395700321000F20038C730C193C972C
IT        0322{       q       b   /
CE44444444FFFFC00440950032103811662
9300000000032200F20388C301C392C081C
Security  0314{   ~           l   p
E88A98AA44FFFFC00A20099038105980968
25349938000314007104300C190C033C574C
```

Each data line is represented in the view in three lines with the first being the character representation of the data line. The second two grayed lines are the hexadecimal values for each character. The topmost line is a guide for identifying column numbers.

The fields are fixed-width and are in the following order. Also shown in the table is the COBOL PICTURE CLAUSE or USAGE of each field.

The cost fields contain nonstandard data.

Field	Column Range	PICTURE CLAUSE or USAGE
Departartment name	1-10	PIC X(10)
Department ID number	11-15	PIC S9(5)
Budget amount	16-19	PIC 9(6) V9(2) COMP
Cost 1	20-23	PIC 9(4) V9(2) COMP-3
Cost 2	24-27	PIC 9(4) V9(2) COMP-3
Cost 3	28-31	PIC 9(4) V9(2) COMP-3
Total cost	32-35	PIC 9(4) V9(2) COMP-3

Resulting Data Set

Output 4.13 PROC PRINT of DEPTCOST Data Set

```
                       Budget and Costs

    Obs      dept         deptid        budget          cost1


     1     Accounting      3040      $1,500.00        $558.21
     2     Shipping        3140      $1,500.00        $535.94
     3     Marketing       3210     $10,000.00        $539.82
     4     IT              3220     $10,000.00      $3,985.80
     5     Security        3140      $5,000.00      $4,039.09


       Obs           cost2            cost3           totcost


        1          $377.98          $291.03        $1,228.22
        2          $438.29          $301.84        $1,276.07
        3        $7,938.08        $1,293.35        $9,771.25
        4        $3,302.11        $3,398.21       $10,686.12
        5        $1,398.01          $539.38        $5,976.48
```

Program

This DATA step reads an external file that was created by a COBOL program. The informats used to read the fields are determined by examining how the COBOL program wrote out the data. See "A Closer Look" for information on determining the informats to use when reading an external file created by a COBOL program.

```
data deptcost;
```

Identify the external file created by the COBOL program.

```
  infile 'myid.deptcost.dat';
```

Read the external file with formatted input.

```
  input @1 dept $10.
        @11 deptid zd5.
        @16 budget ib4.2
        @20 (cost1-cost3) (pd4.2)
        @32 totcost pd4.2;
  format budget cost1-cost3 totcost dollar10.2;
run;
proc print data=deptcost;
  title 'Budget and Costs';
run;
```

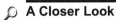 **A Closer Look**

Specifying a SAS Informat Based on the COBOL PICTURE CLAUSE and USAGE

To determine the SAS informats that can read your data, examine the COBOL PICTURE CLAUSE and USAGE statements that created your external file.

COBOL PICTUREs that represent character data use an X to represent the type of data. The length of characters is specified by the number of X's in the PICTURE or by the number enclosed in parentheses. PIC XXX or PIC X(3) use the SAS informat $3. or $CHAR3. to read character data.

The following table shows the informat to select for specific USAGE and PICTURE values:

Usage	Picture	Informat	Width	Decimal
COMP-1	None specified	RB4.		
COMP-2	None specified	RB8.		
DISPLAY	9(int) V9 (fract)	ZD	(int+fract)	(fract)
COMP-3	9(int) V9 (fract)	PD	ceil((int+fract+1)/2)	
COMP	9(int) V9 (fract)	IB	see the following equations	(fract)

The equations that go with the last row in the table follow. In all three situations, the decimal part of the informat is equal to fract.

```
if 1 <= (int + fract) <=4, width is 2.
if 5 <= (int + fract) <=9, width is 4.
if 10 <= (int + fract) <=18, width is 8.
```

COBOL PICTURES that represent numbers use the 9 to represent digits and may use an S to indicate a signed numeric. The V identifies the location of an implied decimal point. The number of digits is either specified by the number of 9's in the picture or by the number enclosed in parentheses. For example, PIC9999V99 is the same as PIC 9(4)V9(2).

The next table presents examples of COBOL specifications of PICTURE and USAGE and the SAS informat that would correctly read the data.

COBOL Specification	SAS Informat
PIC 9(6)V9(2) COMP	IB4.2
PIC 9(7)V99 COMP-3	PD5.2
PIC S9(4)V9(2) DISPLAY	Z6.2

When the PICTURE CLAUSE includes the OCCURS clause, the INPUT statement can be coded as a variable list. For example, the following PICTURE CLAUSE:

```
PIC S9(5)V99 COMP OCCURS 6 TIMES
```

can be coded in an INPUT statement as follows:

```
input  (amt1-amt6) (ib4.2);
```

Specifying Informats

If you are moving the file your COBOL program created from a mainframe to an ASCII system, you may need to use the SAS S370F informats for fields containing nonstandard data, such as packed decimal data. These informats allow you to read data written in EBCDIC from an ASCII system.

To read character data written in EBCDIC from an ASCII system, use the SAS $EBCDICw. informat.

Where to Go From Here

The technical support document TS-642 "Reading EBCDIC Files on ASCII Systems" explains in detail the differences between the EBCDIC and ASCII systems. It addresses reading EBCDIC files on ASCII systems.

For complete documentation on S370 informats and formats, refer to *SAS Language Reference: Dictionary*.

Example 4.14   OpenVMS: Reading an External File Stored on a Tape

Goal

Read an external file from tape where the operating system is OpenVMS.

Strategy

Determine the characteristics of the tape and the file that you want to read from the tape. Issue OpenVMS DCL commands to make the tape available to the SAS session. Submit these commands either before the SAS session starts or from within the SAS session with the SAS X statement.

Define a fileref for the external file on the tape. Define this fileref either with the OpenVMS DEFINE command before the SAS session starts or with the FILENAME SAS statement from within the SAS session.

Write a DATA step to read the tape file. In the INFILE statement, reference the fileref associated with the tape. If the tape is unlabeled, add the RECFM=D and the LRECL= options to the INFILE statement.

Issue OpenVMS commands to release the tape and tape drive when finished reading the external file.

Example Features

This example can execute under the following operating system:

❑ directory-based system (OpenVMS only).

The INPUT statement feature described in this example is the

❑ Double trailing @ (@@)

Other features of this example include:

❑ processing magnetic tapes.

External File

This external file contains census information about several households.

```
10938765MN04045046015012      0065000
93817820MN01028               0056000
93781842MN01056               0225000
39817302MN02064060            0121000
91872058MN03030030005         0052000
81743293MN02035032            0048500
93278182MN0604003901501100900900095000
32982378MN02051050            0042000
83278233MN02055041            0135000
93879278MN01023               0050000
32872383MN02087086            0043000
38237853MN03078075043         0350000
```

This external file contains one data line per household. The data values are aligned in columns and the layout follows.

Field	Column Range
Household ID	1–8
State	9–10
Number of members in the household	11–12
Ages for up to 6 members of the household, 3 columns per age	13–30
Household income	31–37

Resulting Data Set

Output 4.14 CENSUS Data Set

```
                                     Census Data

       h
       o
       u
       s           n
       e           m
       h           e                                              i
       o     s     m                                              n
       l     t     b    a    a     a    a   a   a                 c
   O   d     a     e    g    g     g    g   g   g                 o
   b   i     t     r    e    e     e    e   e   e                 m
   s   d     e     s    1    2     3    4   5   6                 e

   1   10938765   MN    4    45   46    15  12   .    .    $65,000.00
   2   93817820   MN    1    28    .     .   .   .    .    $56,000.00
   3   93781842   MN    1    56    .     .   .   .    .   $225,000.00
   4   39817302   MN    2    64   60     .   .   .    .   $121,000.00
   5   91872058   MN    3    30   30     5   .   .    .    $52,000.00
   6   81743293   MN    2    35   32     .   .   .    .    $48,500.00
   7   93278182   MN    6    40   39    15  11   9    9    $95,000.00
   8   32982378   MN    2    51   50     .   .   .    .    $42,000.00
   9   83278233   MN    2    55   41     .   .   .    .   $135,000.00
  10   93879278   MN    1    23    .     .   .   .    .    $50,000.00
  11   32872383   MN    2    87   86     .   .   .    .    $43,000.00
  12   38237853   MN    3    78   75    43   .   .    .   $350,000.00
```

Program

The following two DATA steps read the same external file from two different tapes under the OpenVMS operating system. The first example shows how to read the external file if it was on a labeled tape. The second example shows how to read the same external file if it was on an unlabeled tape.

The DATA steps under the two situations are identical except for the double trailing @ (@@) that is required in the INPUT statement of the DATA step that reads from an unlabeled tape.

Reading from a Labeled Tape

This section shows the OpenVMS DCL commands you would submit to read an external file from a labeled tape. You can issue these commands either before starting your SAS session or from within your SAS session by using the SAS X statement.

Request that the device known as TAPEDEVICE be allocated to your OpenVMS session.

```
$ ALLOCATE tapedevice
```

Request that the operator mount the labeled tape that has the label CENSUS. (Your OpenVMS session suspends at this command while the operator loads the tape.)

```
$ MOUNT tapedevice census
```

Associate the fileref INDATA with the specific file, CENSUS.DAT, on the tape mounted on TAPEDEVICE.

```
$ DEFINE indata tapedevice:census.dat
```

Invoke a SAS session.

```
$ SAS
```

Include the program into your SAS session or enter the statements.

```
data census;
```

Reference the fileref associated with the external file on tape.

```
   infile indata;
```

Read the data with column input and formatted input.

```
   input householdid 1-8 state $ 9-10 nmembers 11-12
         (age1-age6) (3.) income 31-37;
   format income dollar12.2;
run;
proc print data=census;
   title 'Census Data';
run;
```

Terminate your SAS session.

```
endsas;
```

Unload the tape from TAPEDEVICE.	`$ DISMOUNT tapedevice`
Release the tape drive from the SAS session.	`$ DEALLOCATE tapedevice`

Reading from an Unlabeled Tape

This section shows the OpenVMS DCL commands you would submit to read an external file from an unlabeled tape. You can issue these commands either before starting your SAS session or from within your SAS session by using the SAS X statement.

When you read an external file from an unlabeled tape, you must also add commands and qualifiers to position the tape to the file you want to read. External files on unlabeled tapes do not have filenames and thus cannot be referenced by filename. The example in the previous section was referenced by filename.

Assume that the external file that the DATA step should read is the second on the tape. Assume also that the file is fixed block with a logical record length of 37 bytes and and blocksize of 3700 bytes.

Request that the device known as TAPEDEVICE be allocated to your OpenVMS session.	`$ ALLOCATE tapedevice`
Request that the operator mount an unlabeled tape on TAPEDEVICE. (Your OpenVMS session suspends at this command while the operator loads the tape.) Specify the /FOREIGN qualifier to indicate that the tape is unlabeled. Use a dash to indicate that the command continues to the next line.	`$ MOUNT/FOREIGN -`
Specify the characteristics of the external file with the BLOCKSIZE= and RECORDSIZE= qualifiers.	`/BLOCKSIZE=3700/RECORDSIZE=37 -`
Send a message to the operator with the /ASSIST qualifier. Enter the text of the message with the /COMMENT= qualifier.	`/ASSIST/COMMENT='Please mount CENSUS tape' -`
As required by DCL, end the MOUNT command with the device name.	`tapedevice`

Associate the fileref INDATA with the tape device.	`$ DEFINE indata tapedevice`
Move to the beginning of the tape associated with INDATA by specifying the /REWIND qualifier.	`$ SET MAGTAPE indata/REWIND`
Skip over the first file on the tape to position the tape to the beginning of the second file, which is the file that this example should read.	`$ SET MAGTAPE indata/SKIP=FILES:1`
Invoke a SAS session.	`$ SAS`
Include the program into your SAS session or enter the statements.	`data census;` `   infile indata`
Include the RECFM=D option as required when reading an unlabeled tape.	`        recfm=d`
Include the LRECL= option as required when reading an unlabeled tape. Since this is a fixed blocked file, set the value of the LRECL= option to the logical record length of your tape file.	`        lrecl=37;`
Read the data with column input and formatted input.	`input householdid 1-8 state $ 9-10 nmembers 11-12` `     (age1-age6) (3.) income 31-37`

Add the double trailing @ (@@) to the INPUT statement when reading from a fixed block file on an unlabeled tape.	`     @@;`
	`format income dollar12.2;`
	`run;`

```
proc print data=census;
  title 'Census Data';
run;
```

End the SAS session.

```
endsas;
```

Unload the tape from TAPEDEVICE.

```
$ DISMOUNT tapedevice
```

Release the tape drive from the SAS session.

```
$ DEALLOCATE tapedevice
```

Related Technique #1

When working with *labeled* tapes, you could submit a SAS FILENAME statement from within your SAS session instead of submiting the DCL DEFINE command. The FILENAME statement that replaces the DCL DEFINE command follows.

```
filename indata 'tapedevice:census.dat';
```

Related Technique #2

When working with *unlabeled* tapes, you could submit a SAS FILENAME statement from within your SAS session instead of submitting the DCL DEFINE command. If you submit the FILENAME statement, you must submit the SET MAGTAPE commands after the FILENAME statement.

A way to submit system commands from within a SAS session is with the X SAS statement. The FILENAME statement and the SET MAGTAPE DCL commands submitted from within SAS follow. This code specifies that the tape should be positioned at the beginning of the second file.

```
filename indata 'tapedevice';
x 'set magtape indata/rewind';
x 'set magtape indata/skip=files:1';
```

Related Technique #3

When working with *unlabeled* tapes, you can submit DATA _NULL_ steps to position your tape to a specific external file.

Submit a DATA _NULL_ step for every file you want to skip. To move to the second external file, one DATA _NULL_ step can replace the SET /MAGTAPE commands in the example in "Reading from an Unlabeled Tape".

```
$ ALLOCATE tapedevice
$ MOUNT/FOREIGN -
/BLOCKSIZE=3700/RECORDSIZE=37 -
/ASSIST/COMMENT='Please mount CENSUS tape' -
tapedevice
$ DEFINE indata tapedevice
$ SET MAGTAPE indata/REWIND
$ SAS
```

Completely read the first file on the unlabeled tape, but do not create a data set.

```
data _null_;
```

Specify the RECFM= and LRECL= options even though the file will be skipped. Assume the record length of this first file is 100.

```
   infile indata recfm=d lrecl=100;
   input;
run;
```

Read the second file on the tape and create a data set.

```
data census;
   infile indata recfm=d lrecl=37;
   input householdid 1-8 state $ 9-10 nmembers 11-12
         (age1-age6) (3.) income 31-37 @@;
   format income dollar12.2;
run;
proc print data=census;
   title 'Census Data';
run;
endsas;
$ DISMOUNT tapedevice
$ DEALLOCATE tapedevice
```

🔎 A Closer Look

Specifying the INPUT and INFILE Statements

Your INPUT statements when reading a file from tape generally are written as if reading from a disk file. The exceptions to this are

❐ direct access and keyed access are not allowed

❐ double trailing @ (@@) is required when reading a fixed block file from an unlabeled tape.

When accessing variable-length records, specify the maximum record length as the value of the LRECL= option in the INFILE statement. The minimum value that can be specified for the LRECL= value is 14.

Where to Go From Here

For a more thorough discussion of OpenVMS and magnetic tapes, refer to *SAS Companion for the OpenVMS Environment* and to your OpenVMS documentation. You may also want to consult with your systems programmers on how to use tapes at your site.

Example 4.15   OS/390: Reading an External File Stored on a Tape

Goal

Read an external file from tape where the operating system is OS/390.

Strategy

Determine the characteristics of the tape and the file that you want to read from the tape. Determine the JCL and other requirements necessary at your installation to make a tape available for you to use.

Define a fileref for the external file on the tape. Select the method of defining a fileref based on whether the external file is cataloged or not.

For a cataloged file outside of the SAS session, assign a fileref to the file in the JCL or with a TSO ALLOCATE statement. From within the SAS session, reference a cataloged file explicitly in the FILENAME or INFILE statement.

For an external file that is not cataloged, reference the external file either with a TSO ALLOCATE statement or in the JCL.

Write a DATA step to read the tape file. In the INFILE statement reference the fileref associated with the tape. The DATA step statements can be written as if they are reading from a disk file with the exceptions that direct access and keyed access of an external file on tape are not allowed.

Example Features

This example can execute under the following operating systems:

❐   mainframe (OS/390).

Other features of this example include

❐   processing magnetic tapes.

External File

This external file contains census information about several households.

```
10938765MN04045046015012        0065000
93817820MN01028                 0056000
93781842MN01056                 0225000
39817302MN02064060              0121000
91872058MN03030030005           0052000
81743293MN02035032              0048500
93278182MN0604003901501100900900 95000
32982378MN02051050              0042000
83278233MN02055041              0135000
93879278MN01023                 0050000
32872383MN02087086              0043000
38237853MN03078075043           0350000
```

This external file contains one data line per household. The data values are aligned in columns and the layout follows.

Field	Column Range
Household ID	1–8
State	9–10
Number of members in the household	11–12
Ages for up to 6 members of the Household, 3 columns per age	13–30
Household income	31–37

Resulting Data Set

Output 4.15 PROC PRINT of CENSUS Data Set

```
                              Census Data

        h
        o
        u
        s                n
        e                m
        h                e                                        i
        o    s           m                                        n
        l    t     b     a    a    a    a    a    a                c
   O    d    a     e     g    g    g    g    g    g                o
   b    i    t     r     e    e    e    e    e    e                m
   s    d    e     s     1    2    3    4    5    6                e

   1   10938765   MN   4   45   46   15   12    .    .      $65,000.00
   2   93817820   MN   1   28    .    .    .    .    .      $56,000.00
   3   93781842   MN   1   56    .    .    .    .    .     $225,000.00
   4   39817302   MN   2   64   60    .    .    .    .     $121,000.00
   5   91872058   MN   3   30   30    5    .    .    .      $52,000.00
   6   81743293   MN   2   35   32    .    .    .    .      $48,500.00
   7   93278182   MN   6   40   39   15   11    9    9      $95,000.00
   8   32982378   MN   2   51   50    .    .    .    .      $42,000.00
   9   83278233   MN   2   55   41    .    .    .    .     $135,000.00
  10   93879278   MN   1   23    .    .    .    .    .      $50,000.00
  11   32872383   MN   2   87   86    .    .    .    .      $43,000.00
  12   38237853   MN   3   78   75   43    .    .    .     $350,000.00
```

Program

This DATA step reads an external file from tape under the OS/390 operating system. The first example shows how to read a cataloged external file from tape. The second example shows how to read an uncataloged external file from tape.

You can use the same DATA step whether the external file is cataloged or not. The program that reads the census external file and prints the contents of the CENSUS data set follows.

```
data census;
   infile indata;
   input householdid 1-8 state $ 9-10 nmembers 11-12
         (age1-age6) (3.) income 31-37;
   format income dollar12.2;
run;
proc print data=census;
   title 'Census Data';
run;
```

Reading Cataloged External Files from Tape

This section shows several of the ways that you can define the external file referenced as INDATA in the INFILE statement above.

Within a SAS session, you can define a cataloged external file either in the FILENAME statement or the INFILE statement. The FILENAME statement for the above DATA step follows.

```
filename indata 'myid.census.data' disp=shr;
```

Instead of putting a fileref in the INFILE statement as in the DATA step above, omit the FILENAME statement and explicitly name the file in the INFILE statement as shown below.

```
infile 'myid.census.data';
```

When submitting your program through batch, you can define the fileref with a JCL DD statement. An example of a JCL DD statement that defines a reference to an external file on a standard labeled tape follows. Additionally, the parameters on the second line of this statement can be included, but are not required if the the file is cataloged.

```
//INDATA DD DSN=MYID.CENSUS.DATA,DISP=SHR,
//              UNIT=CART,VOL=SER=999999,LABEL=(,SL)
```

If you are using SAS interactively, you can submit a TSO ALLOCATE statement before submitting the DATA step. The corresponding TSO ALLOCATE command follows.

```
alloc file(indata) da('myid.census.data') shr
```

Reading External Files from Tape that are Not Cataloged

A fileref for an external file on tape that has not been cataloged must be defined outside of SAS with either the JCL DD statement or the TSO ALLOCATE statement. The structure of both these statements is the same as shown in the previous section.

The most common tape format is IBM standard labels (SL). When specifying your JCL DD statement or your TSO ALLOCATE statement to read an IBM standard label tape, include the data set name, UNIT= parameter, volume serial, the label number and type, and disposition.

When the external file is on a nonlabeled tape (NL), the above information must be specified as well as the data control block (DCB) information about the physical characteristics of the tape.

Where to Go From Here

For a more thorough discussion of MVS, TSO, and magnetic tapes, refer to *SAS Companion for the MVS Environment* and to your operating system manuals. You may also want to consult with your systems programmers on how to use tapes at your site.

Example 4.16   UNIX: Reading an External File from Tape

Goal

Read an external file from tape where the operating system is UNIX.

Strategy

Determine the characteristics of the tape and the file that you want to read from the tape. Determine the requirements necessary at your installation to make a tape available for you to use.

Start your SAS session. Submit OPTIONS TAPECLOSE=LEAVE so that no automatic positioning of the tape occurs. Code the UNIX MT command to mount the tape, rewind it, and use it as a norewind device. Enclose the MT command in single quotes and submit it to UNIX with the X SAS statement.

Write a FILENAME statement to define an unnamed pipe to the tape. Specify PIPE as the device type in the FILENAME statement.

Write a DATA step to read the tape file. In the INFILE statement reference the fileref associated with the tape. The DATA step statements can be written as if they are reading from a disk file with the exceptions that direct access and keyed access of an external file on tape are not allowed.

Example Features

This example can execute under the following operating system:

❑   directory-based system (UNIX).

Other features of this example include

❑   processing magnetic tapes.

External File

This external file contains census information about several households.

```
10938765MN04045046015012        0065000
93817820MN01028                 0056000
93781842MN01056                 0225000
39817302MN02064060              0121000
91872058MN03030030005           0052000
81743293MN02035032              0048500
93278182MN0604003901501100090090095000
32982378MN02051050              0042000
83278233MN02055041              0135000
93879278MN01023                 0050000
32872383MN02087086              0043000
38237853MN03078075043           0350000
```

This external file contains one data line per household. The data values are aligned in columns and the layout follows.

Field	Column Range
Household ID	1–8
State	9–10
Number of members in the household	11–12
Ages for up to 6 members of the household, 3 columns per age	13–30
Household income	31–37

Resulting Data Set

Output 4.16 CENSUS Data Set

```
                                        Census Data


            h
            o
            u
            s                  n
            e                  m
            h                  e                                        i
            o     s            m                                        n
            l     t     b  a   a   a   a   a   a                        c
O           d     a     e  g   g   g   g   g   g                        o
b           i     t     r  e   e   e   e   e   e                        m
s           d     e     s  1   2   3   4   5   6                        e


1      10938765   MN    4  45  46  15  12   .   .         $65,000.00
2      93817820   MN    1  28   .   .   .   .   .         $56,000.00
3      93781842   MN    1  56   .   .   .   .   .        $225,000.00
4      39817302   MN    2  64  60   .   .   .   .        $121,000.00
5      91872058   MN    3  30  30   5   .   .   .         $52,000.00
6      81743293   MN    2  35  32   .   .   .   .         $48,500.00
7      93278182   MN    6  40  39  15  11   9   9         $95,000.00
8      32982378   MN    2  51  50   .   .   .   .         $42,000.00
9      83278233   MN    2  55  41   .   .   .   .        $135,000.00
10     93879278   MN    1  23   .   .   .   .   .         $50,000.00
11     32872383   MN    2  87  86   .   .   .   .         $43,000.00
12     38237853   MN    3  78  75  43   .   .   .        $350,000.00
```

Program

This program makes a tape available to SAS and then reads a file from the tape. This program is written to read the second file from an unlabeled tape.

Prevent automatic positioning of the tape by specifying the LEAVE option.

```
options tapeclose=leave;
```

Submit the MT command to UNIX to mount the tape, rewind the tape, and define the tape drive as a no rewind device.

```
x 'mt -t /dev/rmt/0mn rewind';
```

Since this DATA step should read the second file, submit the MT command with the FSF subcommand to skip over the first file and position the tape at the beginning of the second file.

```
x 'mt -t /dev/rmt/0mn fsf 1';
```

Specify the FILENAME statement as a unnamed PIPE, which can pass commands to UNIX. Sending the DD command to UNIX makes the external file on the tape available to SAS.

```
filename indata pipe 'dd if=/dev/rmt/0mn 2> /dev/null';
```

Submit a DATA step to read the external file on tape.

Specify the fileref of the tape in the INFILE statement.

```
data census;

   infile indata;
   input householdid 1-8 state $ 9-10 nmembers 11-12
         (age1-age6) (3.) income 31-37;
   format income dollar12.2;
run;
proc print data=census;
   title 'Census Data';
run;
```

🔍 **A Closer Look**

Specifying the TAPE Device in the FILENAME Statement Instead of PIPE

UNIX more efficiently processes your tape when you define your fileref as an unnamed pipe rather than with the TAPE device. The example above uses an unnamed pipe. If you wanted instead to use the TAPE device, write the FILENAME in the following style.

```
filename indata tape '/dev/rmt/0mn';
```

Processing tapes created on a mainframe

Additional specifications may be required if your external file is on a tape that was created on a mainframe system such as OS/390. UNIX does not support either IBM standard labeled tapes or multivolume tapes. Further, since records are delimited differently on the mainframe compared to an ASCII system such as UNIX, you must also know the DCB characteristics of the file you want to read.

Working with Standard Labeled Tapes

The labels on an IBM standard labeled tape are physical files. For each external file on the tape, there is a label before and after the external file. Since UNIX does not support IBM standard labeled tapes, it views the labels simply as files. Therefore, if you want to read an external file from an IBM standard labeled tape, you must skip over the header label to the beginning of the external file. You can use this formula to determine how many files you should skip over.

```
n_to_skip=(3*external file number) -2
```

As an example, if you wanted to read the third external file from an IBM standard labeled tape, you would skip over 3*3-2=7 files. The command you would submit from your SAS session is:

```
x 'mt -t /dev/rmt/0mn fsf 7';
```

Working with an External File on More Than One Tape

If your external file is on multiple tapes, you must copy the contents of each tape to disk and then concatenate each of the parts in the right order into one file.

Specifying the DCB Characteristics

Because of differences in the way records are stored on UNIX and mainframe systems, you must add to your INFILE statement the DCB characteristics of the external file that you want to read. For example, if the external file in this example was from a tape created on a mainframe and was stored as a fixed block file with logical record length of 37 and block size of 3700, the INFILE statement would look as follows.

```
infile indata recfm=fb lrecl=37 blksize=3700;
```

Where to Go From Here

For a more thorough discussion of UNIX and magnetic tapes, refer to *SAS Companion for the UNIX Environment*, SAS technical report TS-473: "Processing Tapes with the SAS System in the UNIX Environment," and the man pages for your UNIX environment. You may also need to consult with your systems programmers on how to use tapes at your site.

CHAPTER 5
IMPORTING EXTERNAL FILES WITH THE IMPORT WIZARD AND THE EXTERNAL FILE INTERFACE

Introduction

The point-and-click interfaces of the Import Wizard and the External File Interface (EFI) guide you through the steps to read an external file. When you use these facilities, you do not have to enter programming statements to create a data set from an external file. The Import Wizard and EFI are distributed to sites where SAS runs under Windows, UNIX, OpenVMS, and OS/2.

You can access the Import Wizard and EFI through the **Import Data** selection on the File pull-down menu of your SAS session. Although these facilities do not provide support for complex DATA step processing as described in some of examples in this book, they do provide support for many file structures.

An additional feature of the Import Wizard and EFI is that you can save the code that SAS constructs based on your responses to the prompts presented to you by the Import Wizard and EFI.

The Import Wizard can read three standard types of external files:

❐ Comma-separated files where the columns of data values are separated by commas. The default filename extension is CSV, although you can override this default when presented with the file name prompt.

❐ Tab-separated files where the columns of data values are separated by tabs. The default filename extension is TXT, although you can override this default when presented with the file name prompt.

❐ Delimited files where the columns of data values are separated by any delimiter. You specify the delimiter and this delimiter can include the comma or tab as described above. There is no default filename extension for delimited files.

The EFI can read external files where you define through a point-and-click interface the structure of your external file. Some characteristics you can specify with this interface include

- column ranges of your fields

- input style: list or column

- type and length of the field

- number of data lines per observation

- number of data lines to read or write.

If you have a SAS/ACCESS license for a specific database product, you can also use the Import Wizard to read from the database and create a SAS data set. For further information on working with SAS and databases, refer to SAS/ACCESS documentation.

Example 5.1   Reading Delimited Data Values with the Import Wizard

---

Goal

Read an external file by using the Import Wizard. Commas separate the data values in the external file and the filename extension is CSV.

Strategy

Select **Import Data** from the File menu. Select the option to read a comma delimited file. Describe to the wizard other features of your external file by responding to the panels presented. Direct the wizard to submit the code it has built based on your responses.

External File

This external file contains 5 data lines. Each data line contains information about one person and the number of books she read.

```
Neda,0,4,0,3,0,11
Amy,8,3,9,2,4,6
Janet,3,0,12,0,2,1
Pauline,0,1,3,0,4,2
Jo Ann,0,1,0,1,0,1
```

The seven fields in each data line in order are

1. name

2. number of biography books read

3. number of business books read

4. number of fiction books read

5. number of science books read

6. number of self-help books read

7. number of travel books read.

There are no missing data values.

The contents of this external file are identical to that in Example 2.2.

Resulting Data Set

Output 5.1 PROC PRINT of BOOKSREAD Data Set

```
                        Number of Books Read

    Obs     VAR1         VAR2          VAR3          VAR4

     1      Neda          0             4             0
     2      Amy           8             3             9
     3      Janet         3             0            12
     4      Pauline       0             1             3
     5      Jo Ann        0             1             0

    Obs         VAR5          VAR6          VAR7

     1           3             0            11
     2           2             4             6
     3           0             2             1
     4           0             4             2
     5           1             0            11
```

Program

The following displays show the selections made to read an external file with the Import Wizard.

Start the Import Wizard by selecting `Import Data` from the File pull-down menu. Select **`Comma-Separated Values (*.csv)`** as the standard data source. **NOTE:** A file extension of CSV is not required, but by default only those with that filetype are displayed for selection. Select **Next** to move to the next panel.

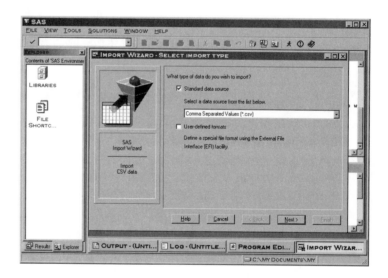

Enter the name of the external file you want to read or select Browse to find the external file you want to read. Select **Options** to set the options specific for this external file.

Deselect Get variable names from first row. By deselecting that choice, SAS automatically sets the value for **First row of data** to 1 since the first row in this external file contains data values not field names. Note that the delimiter selections are grayed out. You are not allowed to select a different delimiter since you specified a CSV external file. Select **OK** to return to the Select File panel. Select **Next** to move to the next panel.

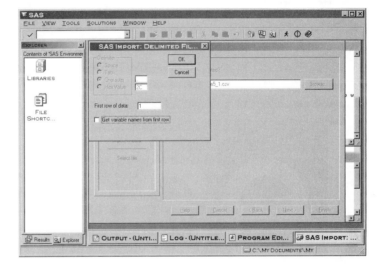

Select a SAS library and enter a data set name. Select **Next** to move to the next panel.

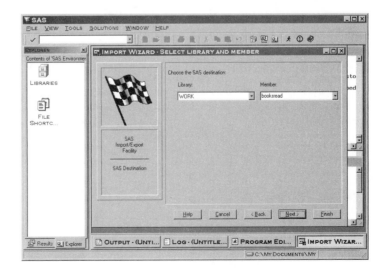

Decide if you want to save the PROC IMPORT code that can read this external file. If so, enter a file name for the program. Select **Finish** to complete the import of the external file. The wizard submits a DATA step to read the external file.

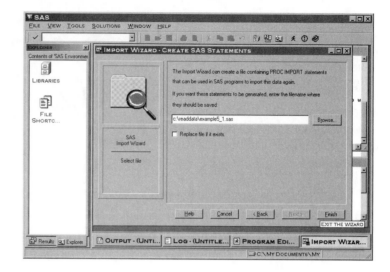

🔍 **A Closer Look**

Reviewing the DATA Step That the Import Wizard Generated to Read the External File

The code that the Import Wizard submitted to read this external file follows.

You can recall the DATA step that the Import Wizard submitted into your Program Editor or Text Editor in your SAS session.

```
164   /*****************************************************
165   *     PRODUCT:     SAS
166   *     VERSION:     8.2
167   *     CREATOR:     External File Interface
168   *     DATE:        17JAN02
169   *     DESC:        Generated SAS Datastep Code
170   *     TEMPLATE SOURCE:  (None Specified.)
171   *****************************************************/
172        data WORK.booksread
;
173      %let _EFIERR_ = 0; /* set the ERROR detection macro
173! variable */
```

The Import Wizard specifies the INFILE statement. It sets the comma as the field delimiter based on your specification and adds the MISSOVER and DSD options. Under Windows, the Import Wizard sets the logical record length of the external file to the maximum of 32767 bytes.

```
174 infile 'C:\readdata\example5_1.csv'
174! delimiter =',' MISSOVER DSD lrecl=32767 ;
```

The Import Wizard evaluates the data lines to determine whether a field is character or numeric and defines the FORMAT, INFORMAT, and INPUT statements accordingly. The Import Wizard assigns variable names sequentially starting with VAR1 when variable names are not provided in the first row of data. See the Closer Look section on limitations of the Import Wizard for more information on setting the length of character variables.

```
175           informat VAR1 $9. ;
176           informat VAR2 best32. ;
177           informat VAR3 best32. ;
178           informat VAR4 best32. ;
179           informat VAR5 best32. ;
180           informat VAR6 best32. ;
181           informat VAR7 best32. ;
182           format VAR1 $9. ;
183           format VAR2 best12. ;
184           format VAR3 best12. ;
185           format VAR4 best12. ;
186           format VAR5 best12. ;
187           format VAR6 best12. ;
188           format VAR7 best12. ;
189      input
190                   VAR1 $
191                   VAR2
192                   VAR3
193                   VAR4
194                   VAR5
195                   VAR6
196                   VAR7
197
;
```

The CALL SYMPUT assigns the value 1 to the macro variable, _EFIERR_, if the automatic variable, _ERROR_, is set to 1 because of an error in reading the data.

```
198      if _ERROR_ then call symput('_EFIERR_',1);
/* set
198! ERROR detection macro variable */
199      run;
```

```
NOTE: Numeric values have been converted to character
      values at the places given by: (Line):(Column).
      198:44
NOTE: The infile 'C:\readdata\example5_1.csv' is:
      File Name=C:\readdata\example5_1.csv,
      RECFM=V,LRECL=32767

NOTE: 5 records were read from the infile
      'C:\readdata\example5_1.csv'.
      The minimum record length was 15.
      The maximum record length was 19.
NOTE: The data set WORK.BOOKSREAD has 5 observations
      and 7 variables.
NOTE: DATA statement used:
      real time              0.05 seconds
```

Submitting the following PROC PRINT step after the DATA step finishes produces the report in Output 5.1:

```
proc print data=booksread;
   title 'Number of Books Read';
run;
```

Limitations of the Import Wizard: Variable Names and Labels

The Import Wizard generates the statements to read your external file. These statements, though, will not likely complete the characterization of your data. You may have to write additional DATA and PROC steps to define meaningful variable names and descriptions. For example, submitting the following PROC DATASETS step after the Import Wizard finishes assigns more meaningful names to the variables in WORK.BOOKSREAD:

```
proc datasets library=work;
   modify family;
   rename var1=biography
          var2=business
          var3=fiction
          var4=science
          var5=selfhelp
          var6=travel;
run;
quit;
```

Lmitations of the Import Wizard: Width Assigned to Character Variables

When SAS creates a data set by using the Import Wizard, it examines a specific number of data lines to determine the attributes of the variables it will create. The default number of data lines that SAS examines in Version 8 is 20. The first 20 data lines may not fully represent your data. For example, if one of your character fields has a data value that is wider than any of those found in the first 20 data lines, then that value will be truncated.

If you want to use the Import Wizard in the situation described above, you can modify the length of the character field one of two ways:

❐ Create the data set through the Import Wizard. After the Import Wizard creates the data set, recall into the program editor window the DATA step that the Import Wizard built, modify the code to define a sufficient length for the character variable, and submit the modified DATA step.

❐ Adjust the SAS default setting **GuessingRows** to a number that includes the data line with the widest data value. To change this setting, enter the SAS Registry Editor by typing **regedit** on the command line. From the Registry **Editor**, expand **Products**, expand **Base**, and select **EFI**. The window on the right contains settings for the EFI. Double-click **GuessingRows**, enter the new value, and press **OK**, and close the Registry Editor window.

Specifying the Data Source

You can choose from several types of standard data sources when reading an external file with the Import Wizard. These choices are presented to you on the first screen when you select **Import Data** from the File menu. The three choices that read external files are

❑ **Delimited File (*.*)**

❑ **Comma Separated Values (*.csv)**

❑ **Tab Delimited Files (*.txt).**

The three differ on the default delimiter that separates fields in the data line. The first, Delimited File, defaults to a space, but you can also change the delimiter to another character in the Options window. When you select either a CSV or a TXT file, you cannot change the delimiter in the options window.

The three also differ on the list of files presented from which you can choose the external file that the Import Wizard should read. All files are included in the list when you select **Delimited File**. When you select **Comma Separated Values**, only files with the extension .CSV are presented for selection. When you select **Tab Delimited Files**, only files with the extension TXT are presented for selection.

Related Technique

Although the code that the Import Wizard submits to read your external file is a DATA step, the code it saves for you to use is a PROC IMPORT step.

The PROC IMPORT step that the Import Wizard saved for this example follows.

Name the output data set.

```
PROC IMPORT OUT= WORK.booksread
```

Name the external file.

```
           DATAFILE= "C:\readdata\example5_1.csv"
```

Declare that the data values are separated with commas by specifying CSV as the value for the DBMS= option.

```
           DBMS=CSV
```

Indicate that SAS can overwrite the data set if it already exists.

```
           REPLACE;
```

Indicate that SAS should not read variable names from the external file.

```
        GETNAMES=NO;
```

Specify the data line where SAS should begin reading from the external file.

```
        DATAROW=1;
RUN;
```

Where to Go From Here

For more complete information on PROC IMPORT, refer to *SAS Procedures Guide*.

Example 5.2   Reading Delimited Data Values with the External File Interface (EFI)

Goal

Read an external file by using the External File Interface (EFI). Specify to the EFI the properties of the variables you want it to define. Spaces separate the data values in the external file.

Strategy

Select **Import Data** from the File menu. Select the type of data that you want to import as **User-defined formats**. Describe to the EFI other features of your external file by responding to the panels presented. Direct the wizard to submit the code it has built based on your responses.

External File

This external file contains expense information for four employees.

```
A03885 HR 1039.65 543.87 109.83 257.45
A03918 Acctg 3029.98 837.00 . 362.91
A05291 . . . . .
A06573 IT 5603.81 2091.23 393.39 103.95
```

The six fields in each data line in order are:

1. employee id

2. department

3. hardware expense

4. software expense

5. books expense

6. supplies expense.

The fields are separated by spaces and are not column aligned. A period (.) represents a missing value.

In the third data line, the employee id is the only information recorded.

The contents of this external file are identical to that in Example 2.1.

Resulting Data Set

Output 5.2 PROC PRINT of EXPENSES Data Set

```
Expenses by Employee Data Set Created by User-Defined Format

Obs  personid  dept   hardware   software     books   supplies

1    A03885    HR     $1039.65   $543.87    $109.83   $257.45
2    A03918    Acctg  $3029.98   $837.00              $362.91
3    A05291
4    A06573    IT     $5603.81   $2091.23   $393.39   $103.95
```

Program

The following displays show the selections made to read an external file with the EFI. The initial three displays use the Import Wizard.

Start the EFI by selecting `Import Data` from the File menu. Select **`User-defined formats`** as the type of data to import. Select **Next** to move to the next panel.

Specify the external file that you want to read by either: selecting `Browse` to find the external file you want to read from a list of files, or by entering the specific name of the external file you want to read. Select **Next** to move to the next panel. Note that the **Options** button is grayed out. You will be allowed to enter file specific information later.

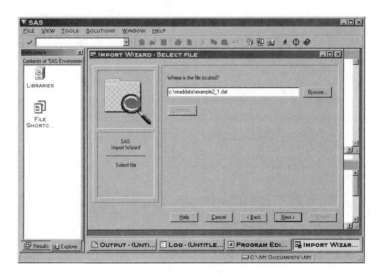

Select the WORK library and enter the name of the data set you want to create. Select `Next` to move to the next panel.

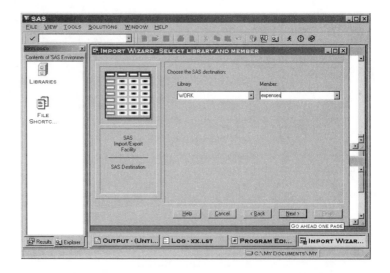

Select `Finish` to start up the EFI so that you can describe the fields in the external file.

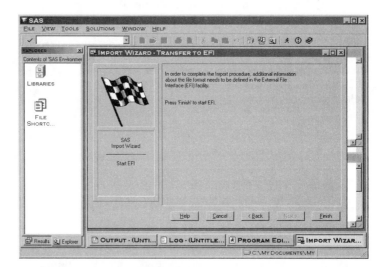

View the contents of the external file in the upper left of the the Import:List window. View the contents of the resulting SAS data set in the upper right box. Observe that initially the SAS data set is empty. Observe that the lower part of the window provides you with fields to enter information about the data values. Select the **Options** button to open an additional panel in which you can specify additional information about the external file.

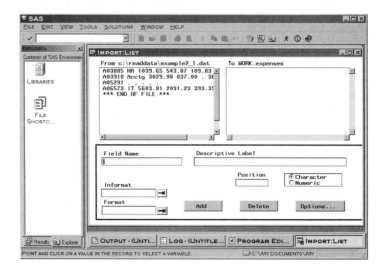

Review the default settings of the options to determine if any should be changed to read the external file. For this example, keep the space as the delimiter between fields. Select **OK** to close the Options for Import window.

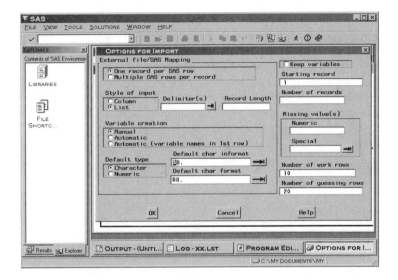

In the Import: List window, describe each field in the external file one at a time. Set the first field in the data line to be the character variable PERSONID. Enter a descriptive label for PERSONID. Do not enter any additional informat or format information so that the default informat and format of $8., which were set in the Options for Import window, are used. Enter the position in the data line that PERSONID occupies. Press ENTER to view how SAS will read the data lines.

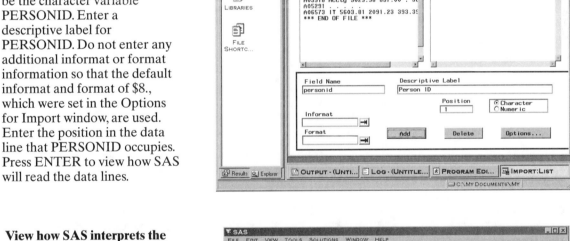

View how SAS interprets the way you defined PERSONID; the values SAS intends to assign to the variable PERSONID are highlighted. Note that EFI fills in the informat and format fields with their default values. Since the interpretation is correct, press the **Add** button to accept the definition of PERSONID.

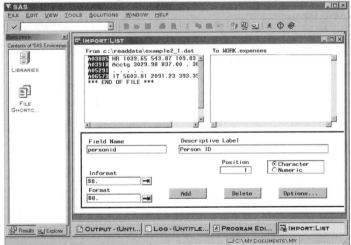

View the values of PERSONID in the upper right box. Observe the processing message that the EFI wrote in the lower left message area.

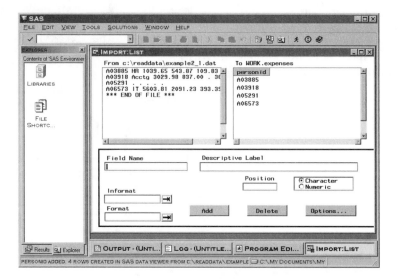

Enter the information for the second variable, DEPT. Define these characteristics for DEPT: character, position 2, informat of $8. and format of $8. Press ENTER to view how the EFI defines the variable DEPT. Press **Add** to add the DEPT field to the SAS data set.

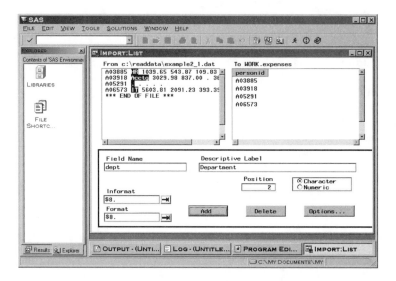

Verify that the EFI adds the variable DEPT to WORK.EXPENSES. Notice that the EFI correctly read a missing value for DEPT from the third data line.

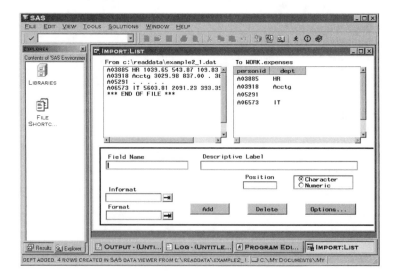

Enter the information for the third variable, HARDWARE.
Define these characteristics for HARDWARE: numeric, position 3, informat of 8., and format of dollar8.2. Press ENTER to view how the EFI defines the variable HARDWARE. Press the arrow to the right of the format specification to select DOLLAR from the format list.

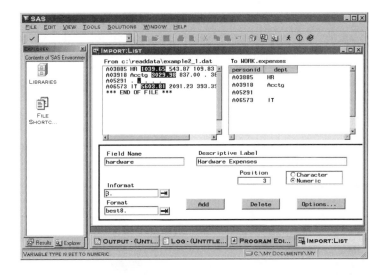

Select the DOLLAR format and enter the width and decimal values in the entry boxes on the right. Press OK to return to the previous window. From that window, press **Add** to add HARDWARE to the data set.

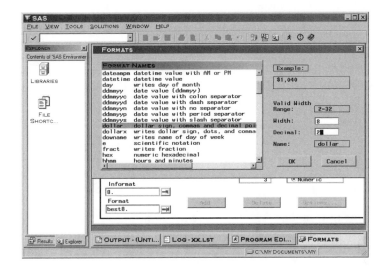

Verify that you added HARDWARE correctly.
Notice that SAS applied the DOLLAR format to the values of HARDWARE and that a missing value is shown for the value of HARDWARE for the third observation.

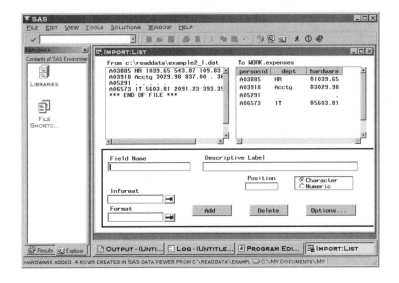

Enter the information for the remaining fields in the external file. This table shows the information specified to create the variables.

SAS Variable Name	Descriptive Label	Position	Type	Informat	Format
software	Software Expenses	4	Numeric	8.	DOLLAR8.2
books	Books Expenses	5	Numeric	8.	DOLLAR8.2
supplies	Supplies Expenses	6	Numeric	8.	DOLLAR8.2

View in the upper right box the values of the last three variables. Save the data in the WORK.EXPENSES data set by selecting **Save** from the File menu. Exit the EFI by closing the window.

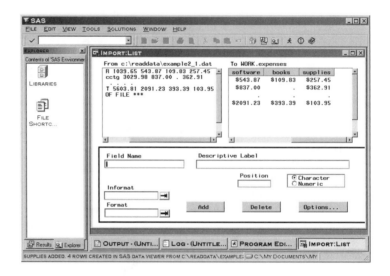

Look for the note in the SAS log that confirms that the data set was created.

```
NOTE: WORK.EXPENSES was successfully created.
```

🔍 **A Closer Look**

Reviewing the DATA Step that the EFI Used to Read the External File

The DATA step that the EFI submits to read this external file follows.

View the DATA step that the EFI submitted to read your external file either by saving the SAS source from within the EFI or by recalling the program into your Program Editor or Text Editor after you exit the EFI.

```
/*************************************************************
*    PRODUCT:    SAS
*    VERSION:    8.2
*    CREATOR:    External File Interface
*    DATE:       17JAN02
*    DESC:       Generated SAS Datastep Code
*    TEMPLATE SOURCE:  (None Specified.)
*************************************************************/
    data WORK.expenses        ;
    %let _EFIERR_ = 0; /* set the ERROR detection macro
                            variable */
```

The EFI specifies the INFILE statement. It sets the space as the field delimiter based on your specification and it includes the MISSOVER and DSD options.

```
infile 'C:\readdata\example2_1.dat'
        delimiter = ' ' MISSOVER DSD  ;
```

The EFI uses the variable names, informats, formats, and labels that you specified.

```
        informat personid $8. ;
        informat dept $8. ;
        informat hardware 8. ;
        informat software 8. ;
        informat books 8. ;
        informat supplies 8. ;
        format personid $8. ;
        format dept $8. ;
        format hardware dollar8.2 ;
        format software dollar8.2 ;
        format books dollar8.2 ;
        format supplies dollar8.2 ;
        label personid="Person ID";
        label dept="Department";
        label hardware="Hardware Expenses";
        label software="Software Expenses";
        label books="Books Expenses";
        label supplies="Supplies Expenses";
input
                personid $
                dept $
                hardware
                software
                books
                supplies
        ;
        if _ERROR_ then call symput('_EFIERR_',1);  /* set
ERROR detection macro variable */
        run;
```

Advantages of Specifying a User-Defined Format to the Import Wizard

When specifying a user-defined format, you can request that only certain fields and data lines be read from the external file and you can specify properties of the variables that result. If instead you selected a standard data source, as in Example 5.1, all fields and all data lines are read from the external file. Meaningful names and attributes are not assigned to the variables.

Saving the Code Generated by the EFI

When you specify a user-defined format, you are not presented with a panel that lets you save code to read in the external file as you are when you use the Import Wizard as in Example 5.1. You can, however, save the DATA step that the EFI submitted one of two ways:

❑ While still in the EFI, select **View SAS Source** from the Edit menu. From the window that is displaying the SAS source, select one of the three Save options to save your code: **Save**, **Save as**, **Save as file**.

❑ After exiting the EFI, you can recall the DATA step into the Program Editor or Text Editor and then save the code to a file.

CHAPTER 6
USING ACCESS METHODS AND THE XML LIBNAME ENGINE TO READ DATA

Introduction

In addition to reading from physical files, SAS can read data from devices on other systems. SAS uses access methods to read this type of data. SAS treats the data it reads with an access method as if it were in an external file.

Access methods are usually specific to the operating environment. This chapter presents examples of the following access methods:

Access Method	Description	Example
CATALOG	Read from a SAS catalog.	6.4
DDE	Read from a Windows application by using Dynamic Data Exchange (DDE).	6.5
FTP	Read from a file from any host machine that is connected to a network with an FTP server running.	6.1, 6.2
SOCKET	Read from a Transmission Control Protocol/Internet Protocol(TCP/IP) socket.	6.3
URL	Read from a file on anyhost machine that is connected to a network with a Univeral Resource Locator (URL) server running.	6.6

SAS can also read a variety of extensible markup language (XML) documents with the XML LIBNAME engine. Example 6.7 presents an example of reading an XML document with the XML LIBNAME engine.

Example 6.1 Reading from an External File Stored on a Remote Host with the FTP Access Method

Goal

From a local SAS session, read an external file stored on a remote host system without downloading the external file. Use file transfer protocol (FTP) to read the external file.

Strategy

Identify with the FILENAME statement the external file stored on the remote host. Specify the FTP keyword in the FILENAME statement to indicate that you will use the FTP access method.

Write a DATA step to read the external file. Reference in the INFILE statement the fileref assigned to the remote external file.

External File

This external file contains a list of students for an advisor in the Biology department.

```
2393834873Keen, Kerry              Genetics       2003
2836183495Lindsay, Nancy           Microbiology   2004
2838378510Lee, Lois                Genetics       2004
2903895839Carlson, Gina            Cell Biology   2005
2918387281Rhodes, Richard          Cell Biology   2004
2938281731Woski, Donna             Genetics       2004
3293832921Anderson, Robert         Microbiology   2005
3728437267Roscoe, Marie Louise     Genetics       2005
3927823853Bates, Joey              Cell Biology   2005
3982748372Gomez Jr., Ed            Microbiology   2006
```

The data values are aligned in columns and the layout follows.

Field	Column Range
Student ID	1–10
Student name	11–34
Student major	35–49
Expected graduation year	50–53

Resulting Data Set

Output 6.1 STUDENTS Data Set

```
                              Student List

      Obs     studentid   studentname                major        gradyear

        1     2393834873   Keen, Kerry                Genetics        2003
        2     2836183495   Lindsay, Nancy             Microbiology    2004
        3     2838378510   Lee, Lois                  Genetics        2004
        4     2903895839   Carlson, Gina              Cell Biology    2005
        5     2918387281   Rhodes, Richard            Cell Biology    2004
        6     2938281731   Woski, Donna               Genetics        2004
        7     3293832921   Anderson, Robert           Microbiology    2005
        8     3728437267   Roscoe, Marie Louise       Genetics        2005
        9     3927823853   Bates, Joey                Cell Biology    2005
       10     3982748372   Gomez Jr., Ed              Microbiology    2006
```

Program

This program reads an external file stored on a UNIX remote host using the FTP access method. The program executes from a local Windows SAS session. The external file remains on the remote host.

Assign a fileref to the external file on the remote host. Follow the fileref with the access method.

```
filename myfile ftp
```

Specify the name of the external file on the remote host and enclose the name in quotation marks.

```
                    'example6_1'
```

Specify the user's id on the remote host.

```
                    user='myid'
```

Instruct SAS to prompt you for the password for the user account on the remote host when SAS executes this FILENAME statement.
(Specify the PASS= option with the password enclosed in quotes if it is acceptable to include the password in the program code.)

```
                    prompt
```

Identify the network name of the remote host where the FTP server is running. Specify the value as either the name of the server or the IP address of the server (e.g. 999.99.99) .

```
                         host='biology.univ.edu'
```

Specify the directory of the remote external file.

```
                    cd='/students/biology/advisors';
data students;
  infile myfile;
```

Reference the fileref associated with the external file stored on the remote host.

Read the data with column input.

```
    input studentid 1-10 studentname $ 11-34 major $ 35-49
          gradyear 50-53;
run;
proc print data=students;
  title 'Student List';
run;
```

System-specific Information

The FILENAME statement in this example is specific to the operating system. Examples of specifying a similar FILENAME statement for other operating environments follow.

OpenVMS

```
filename myfile ftp 'example6_1.dat' user='myid' prompt
         host='biology.univ.edu'
         cd='[students.biology.advisors]';
```

OS/390

```
filename myfile ftp
         'students.biology.advisors.example61'
         user='myid' prompt host='biology.univ.edu';
```

Windows

```
filename myfile ftp 'example6_1' user='myid' prompt
         host='biology.univ.edu'
         cd='c:\students\biology\advisors';
```

A Closer Look

Availability of the FTP Access Method

The FTP access method is part of Base SAS. You do not have to license additional products such as SAS/CONNECT to use the FTP access method.

Example 6.2   Reading Multiple Files Stored on a Remote Host with the FTP Access Method

Goal

From a local SAS session, execute one DATA step that reads several external files stored on a remote host system. Use file transfer protocol (FTP) to read the external files. The external files have the same naming convention.

Strategy

Specify with a FILENAME statement the files to read from the remote host. Follow the fileref with the FTP keyword and the file specification. Follow the file specification with the MGET keyword to tell SAS that multiple files may be read.

For the external file part of the FILENAME statement, specify that only files whose names contain specific text be read. Generalize the specification by using wildcard characters as appropriate to represent possible characters at a particular position in the filename.

Include in the FILENAME statement information about the remote host connection and directory. Identify the host name or IP address with the HOST= option. Specify the remote host userid with the USER= option. Indicate with the PROMPT keyword that you want the remote host to prompt you for the password to connect to the remote host. Specify the directory of the files with the CD= option.

Write a DATA step to read the files. Reference in the INFILE statement the fileref defined in the FILENAME statement. Define a variable with the EOV= option in the INFILE statement. Test this variable's value so that specific statements can be executed when its value is **1**, which is when SAS is reading the first data line in a file. Reset the EOV= variable to **0** after detecting the first data line in a file so that the program can determine when the first data line in the next file is read.

Define a variable with the FILENAME= option in the INFILE statement. Extract information from the value of this variable so that information about the external file can be retained in the output data set.

External File

This is the list of files in the /students/biology/general directory.

```
LewisCA1
LewisCA3
LewisCA4
LewisCA10
OlsenGG2
OlsenGG5
RogersTO6
SmithRA7
YoungCM8
YoungCM9
YoungCM11
```

There are 11 files in this directory. Each file represents one section of the general biology course and contains the names of the students in the section. The course has five instructors and eleven sections.

The name of each file starts with the instructor's name: last name first followed by the first and middle initials. The numeric suffix on the filename indicates the section number of the course.

External Files

The program reads the two external files for instructor GG Olsen. The content of these two files is displayed.

```
3453283471Morris, Susan         88
3727823711Chang, David          77
3821872813Press, Jill           94
3827375938Monroe, Norris        98
3827376218Thorson, Robert       85
3827821739Simon, Lena           81
3831873285Leslie, David         89
3938282818Banks, Mindy         100

3273619371Andrews, Susan        82
3384572671Boston, Betsy        100
3388173948Newly, Neil           90
3457328372Ramirez, Eduardo     100
3727661183Gardner, Sharon       95
3817375923Fields, Elaine        81
3827372192Van Pelt, Rosa        89
3827395928Dixon, Matt           96
3837279187Smith, Chuck          79
3958382938Boxer, Gail           85
```

The names and grades for each of the students in Olsen's two sections are listed above. The first group of eight students are from Section 2. The second group of 10 students are from Section 5.

The data values are aligned in columns and the layout follows.

Field	Column Range
Student ID	1–10
Student name	11–29
Grade	30–32

Resulting Data Set

Output 6.2 PROC PRINT of STUDENTS Data Set

```
                           Olsen's Students

        Obs     section     studentid      studentname      grade

         1         2        3453283471    Morris,  Susan       88
         2         2        3727823711    Chang,  David        77
         3         2        3821872813    Press,  Jill         94
         4         2        3827375938    Monroe,  Norris      98
         5         2        3827376218    Thorson,  Robert     85
         6         2        3827821739    Simon,  Lena         81
         7         2        3831873285    Leslie,  David       89
         8         2        3938282818    Banks,  Mindy       100
         9         5        3273619371    Andrews,  Susan      82
        10         5        3384572671    Boston,  Betsy      100
        11         5        3388173948    Newly,  Neil         90
        12         5        3457328372    Ramirez,  Eduardo   100
        13         5        3727661183    Gardner,  Sharon     95
        14         5        3817375923    Fields,  Elaine      81
        15         5        3827372192    Van Pelt,  Rosa      89
        16         5        3827395928    Dixon,  Matt         96
        17         5        3837279187    Smith,  Chuck        79
        18         5        3958382938    Boxer,  Gail         85
```

Program

This program reads several external files stored on a UNIX remote host using the FTP access method. The program executes from a local Windows SAS session.

Assign a fileref to the external files on the remote host. Follow the fileref with the access method.

```
filename instructor ftp
```

Use wildcard notation to specify the files to read from the remote host. Read all files that start with OlsenGG.

```
    'OlsenGG*'
```

Indicate that multiple files may be read.

```
   mget
```

Specify the user's id on the remote host.

```
  user='myid'
```

Instruct SAS to prompt you for the password for the user account on the remote host when SAS executes this FILENAME statement. (Specify the PASS= option with the password enclosed in quotes if it is acceptable to include the password in the program code.)

```
                              prompt
```

Identify the network name of the remote host where the FTP server is running. Specify the value as either the name of the server or the IP address of the server (e.g. 999.99.99) .

```
                    host='biology.univ.edu'
```

Specify the directory of the remote external files.

```
               cd='/students/biology/general';
```

```
data students;
```

Define the variable HOSTEXFILE to hold the name of the external file.

```
   length hostexfile $ 50;
```

Reference the fileref associated with the external files stored on the remote host.

```
infile instructor
```

Define a variable to hold the name of the file currently being read by the DATA step.

```
      filename=hostexfile
```

Define a variable whose value is set to 1 when SAS reads the first data line in a file.

```
      eov=firstrec;
```

Retain the variable SECTION whose value remains constant for all data lines read from an external file.

```
retain section;
```

Drop this variable since it is only needed for the duration of the DATA step.

```
drop num;
```

Read the data with column input.

```
input studentid 1-10 studentname $ 11-29 grade 30-32;
```

Execute this DO block when SAS reads the first data line in an external file.

```
if _n_=1 or firstrec then do;
```

Extract the numeric suffix of the filename and assign it to the variable SECTION.

```
      num=indexc(hostexfile,'0123456789');
      section=input(substr(hostexfile,num),best3.);
```

Reset the variable named on the EOV= option to 0 so that it can detect when the first data line in the next external file is read.

```
      firstrec=0;
   end;
run;
proc print data=students;
  title 'Olsen''s Students';
run;
```

System-Specific Information

The FILENAME statement in this example is specific to the operating system. Examples of specifying a similar FILENAME statement for other operating environments follow.

OpenVMS

```
filename myfile ftp 'olsengg*.dat' mget user='myid'
         prompt
         host='biology.univ.edu'
         cd='[students.biology.general]';
```

OS/390

```
filename instructor ftp
         'students.biology.general.olsengg*' mget
         user='myid' prompt host='biology.univ.edu';
```

Windows

```
filename instructor ftp 'OlsenGG*.dat' mget user='myid'
         host='biology.univ.edu' prompt
         cd='c:\students\biology\general';
```

A Closer Look

Understanding the EOV= Option in This Example

The EOV= INFILE statement option defines a variable whose value is set to **1** when the first data line in a series of files is read. SAS sets the variable to **1** only after it encounters the next external file. When SAS processes the first file in the series, the value of the EOV= variable is **0**.

Execution of the INPUT statement causes SAS to evaluate the EOV= condition. A test of the value of the EOV= variable, therefore, should follow the INPUT statement.

Once the EOV= variable is set to **1**, it remains **1** unless you reset the value. Therefore, if you want to detect when SAS reads the first data line in subsequent files, you must reset the value of the EOV= variable to **0** after SAS sets it to **1**.

In this example, when the first external file is accessed by the INFILE statement, the value of FIRSTREC is **0**. When the IF-THEN block is executed the first time, the value of FIRSTREC is **0**. To define a section for observations from the first file, the test of whether the DATA step is on its first iteration (**_n_=1**) must be included on the IF statement.

Availability of the FTP Access Method

The FTP access method is part of Base SAS. You do not have to license additional products such as SAS/CONNECT to use the FTP access method.

Example 6.3   Transmitting Data Between SAS Applications through a TCP/IP Socket

Goal

Establish a TCP/IP connection so that a local SAS session operating in server mode can receive data transmitted from another SAS application through a TCP/IP socket and create a SAS data set.

Strategy

Specify a FILENAME statement for the local SAS session that defines the local session as the server. Include the keyword SOCKET and the port number of the socket in the FILENAME statement.

Write a DATA step that you submit from the local SAS session to listen for the client application on the remote session. Specify an INFILE statement with the fileref defined for the local SAS session. Define a variable with the EOV= option in the INFILE statement that SAS sets to **1** when reading the first line in a file. When this variable's value is **1**, a connection has been made by the client application.

On the remote SAS session, specify a FILENAME statement with the keyword SOCKET and the port number that the server application listens to for a connection. Write a DATA step that writes data from selected observations to the local session. Specify in the FILE statement in the DATA step the fileref for the TCP/IP socket.

Remote SAS Data Set

Output 6.3a PROC PRINT of MACHINES Data Set on Remote Session

```
                            Recent Purchases

       Obs     type                    id          purchasedate

         1     Computer            A0031934Z3        04/03/2002
         2     Scanner             UI3097Y009        04/15/2002
         3     Photocopier         C93810691E        05/01/2002
         4     Laser Printer       TY03120591        05/03/2002
         5     Computer            B8372968RE        05/10/2002
         6     Monitor             PN9284TU36        05/18/2002
         7     Paper Shredder      JK372834T3        05/20/2002
         8     Computer            WQ096821RR        05/21/2002
         9     Fax Machine         II93820RW3        05/22/2002
        10     Digital Camera      RW320482V9        05/29/2002
```

Resulting Local SAS Data Set

Output 6.3b PROC PRINT of PROC PRINT of COMPUTERS Data Set

```
                        Recent Purchases: Computers

         Obs        type            id          purchasedate


          1       Computer      A0031934Z3       04/03/2002
          2       Computer      B8372968RE       05/10/2002
          3       Computer      WQ096821RR       05/21/2002
```

Program

The objective of this program is to transmit data through a TCP/IP socket from a remote SAS session to a local SAS session. The remote SAS session acts as the client and executes a DATA step that writes data to the socket. The local SAS session acts as the server and waits to receive data over a TCP/IP socket. The local SAS session executes a DATA step that reads the data transmitted over the socket.

The code submitted from the local SAS session, the server, follows. This DATA step must be submitted before the DATA step on the client is submitted. This DATA step does not execute completely until the TCP/IP connection has been made.

Assign a fileref to the TCP/IP socket connection. Follow the fileref with the access method.

```
filename local socket
```

Specify the port number.

```
          ':9999'
```

Define the TCP/IP socket as a listening socket, thus treating the local session as a server.

```
          server
```

Set the maximum number of connections that the server will accept.

```
          reconn=3;
```

Specify the fileref of the TCP/IP socket connection.

```
data computers;
    infile local
```

Define a variable that SAS sets to 1 when reading the first line from an external file. In this situation, SAS sets this variable to **1** when the TCP/IP connection is made.

```
          eov=newconnect;
```

Read the data transmitted over the socket from the client SAS session. Read the data with formatted input.

```
input type $15. +1 id $10. +1 purchasedate mmddyy10.;
```

Write a message to the SAS log when the value of the EOV= variable is 1, which indicates that a TCP/IP connection has been made.

```
     if newconnect then put 'new connection received';
  run;
```

The code submitted from the remote SAS session, the server, follows. Assume that the server IP address is SYSX.UNX.ABCCO.COM.

Define a fileref for the client side of the connection.

```
filename remote
```

Specify the access method.

```
     socket
```

Specify the host and port number of the connection. Follow the host information with a colon and the port number defined on the first FILENAME statement.

```
     'sysx.unx.abcco.com:9999';
```

Select observations where type='Computer'.

```
data _null_;
  set machines(where=(type='Computer'));
```

Write to the location identified by the fileref REMOTE. In this example, REMOTE is the 9999 socket connecting to the SYSX.UNX.ABCCO.COM host.

```
  file remote;
```

Write the data values to the socket that the first DATA step then reads, which creates the COMPUTERS data set on the local SAS session.

```
  put type $15. +1 id $10. +1 purchasedate mmddyy10.;
run;
```

🔍 **A Closer Look**

Understanding the Connections that Can Be Made with the Socket Access Method

You are not limited to communication between SAS sessions with the socket access method. For example, you might have an application in another software package that writes data to a socket as does the remote SAS DATA step above. Your local SAS session could then read this transmitted data into a SAS data set as in the example.

With the SOCKET access method, SAS can act as either the client or server when communicating with another application. Furthermore, the client and server applications can reside on the same machine or on different machines that are connected by a network.

Specifying the port number

Typically, servers use well-known ports to listen for connections. These port numbers are reserved by the system for specific server applications. For more information about how well-known ports are defined on your system, refer to the documentation for your TCP/IP software or ask your system administrator.

Availability of the socket access method

The socket access method is part of Base SAS. You do not have to license additional products such as SAS/CONNECT to use the socket access method. You do, however, need to know about the availability of ports on your system.

Where to Go From Here

Refer to *SAS Language Reference: Dictionary*, for more information on this access method. Your host-specific SAS Companion provides more detailed information on using this access method under your operating system.

Example 6.4   Reading an Entry from a SAS Catalog

Goal

Read the contents of a SOURCE entry from a catalog, update the information in the entry, and write the revised information to a new entry.

Strategy

Identify with a FILENAME statement the catalog entry that the program should read.

Write a DATA _NULL_ step to read the catalog entry and find the text that needs to be modified. Write a new catalog entry copying the unchanged information from the entry that is read and incorporating the newly updated information.

Existing Catalog Source Entry

The entry MYFORMATS.SOURCE contains a PROC FORMAT step.

```
proc format;
   value $inits 'MMD'='Margaret M. Dean           '
                'AEK'='Andrea Elizabeth King      '
                'JAR'='John A. Ross               '
                'SST'='Susan S. Thompson          ';
run;
```

Resulting Catalog Source Entry

The DATA _NULL_ step creates the source entry NEWFORMATS.SOURCE.

```
proc format;
   value $inits 'MMD'='Margaret M. Dean           '
                'AEY'='Andrea Elizabeth Young     '
                'JAR'='John A. Ross               '
                'SST'='Susan S. Thompson          ';
run;
```

This entry contains the same information as in MYFORMATS.SOURCE with the exception of the modified initials and last name for Andrea Elizabeth King.

Program

This program reads a source entry from a catalog, modifies specific values, and creates a new source entry in the same catalog.

Assign a fileref to the catalog source entry. Follow the fileref with the access method.

```
filename oldprog catalog
```

Identify the catalog and source entry you want to read.

```
                'mycompany.programs.myformats.source';
```

Specify the access method after the fileref.

```
filename newprog catalog
```

Identify the catalog and source entry you want to create.

```
                              'mycompany.programs.newformats.source';
```

Identify the input source entry.

Prevent the INPUT statement from moving to the next data line if the current data line is not as wide as the INPUT statement expects.

```
data _null_;
   infile oldprog
          truncover;
```

Preserve the layout of each input data line by using the $CHAR*w*. informat.

```
input programline $char100.;
```

Find the data line in the source entry that should be updated and modify the contents of the data line.

```
findaek=index(programline,'AEK');
if findaek > 0 then do;
  substr(programline,findaek,3)='AEY';
  findln=index(programline,'King');
  if findln > 0 then
     substr(programline,findln,5)='Young';
end;
```

Identify the output source entry.

```
file newprog;
```

Preserve the layout that was read in by writing out the variable with the $CHAR*w*. format.

```
put @1 programline $char100.;
run;
```

Example 6.5   Reading a Microsoft Excel Worksheet with DDE

Goal

Create a SAS data set by reading the content of an Microsoft Excel worksheet. Use the DDE access method so that SAS can directly read the contents of the worksheet.

Strategy

Specify in the FILENAME statement that the access method is DDE. Include in the FILENAME statement the DDE triplet that identifies the worksheet and the rows and columns to be read from the worksheet.

Make sure Microsoft Excel is running with the worksheet open before submitting a DATA step to read the contents of the worksheet. In the INFILE statement, reference the fileref defined in the FILENAME statement.

Existing Microsoft Excel Spreadsheet

The two worksheets in this workbook contain information for a blood chemistry measurement for 12 patients over a four week period. This screen shows the data for Group A.

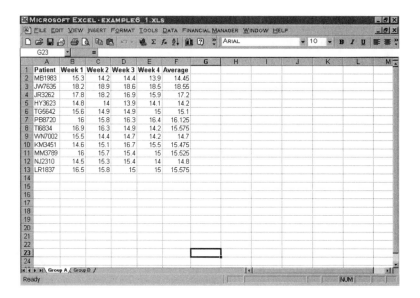

Resulting SAS Data Set

Output 6.5 PROC PRINT of GROUPA Data Set

```
                           Patient Data for Group A

     Obs   Patient   Week_1   Week_2   Week_3   Week_4   Average

      1    MB1983     15.3     14.2     14.4     13.9     14.450
      2    JW7635     18.2     18.9     18.6     18.5     18.550
      3    JR3262     17.8     18.2     16.9     15.9     17.200
      4    HY3623     14.8     14.0     13.9     14.1     14.200
      5    TG5642     15.6     14.9     14.9     15.0     15.100
      6    PB8720     16.0     15.8     16.3     16.4     16.125
      7    TI6834     16.9     16.3     14.9     14.2     15.575
      8    WN7002     15.5     14.4     14.7     14.2     14.700
      9    KM3451     14.6     15.1     16.7     15.5     15.475
     10    MM3789     16.0     15.7     15.4     15.0     15.525
     11    NJ2310     14.5     15.3     15.4     14.0     14.800
     12    LR1837     16.5     15.8     15.0     15.0     15.575
```

Program

This program reads the rows in a Microsoft Excel worksheet. SAS reads the data directly from the worksheet by using the DDE access method.

The worksheet must be open before you submit the program.

Define a fileref for the worksheet. Follow the fileref with the access method.

```
filename patients dde
```

Specify the DDE triplet. Include in the triplet the software application, the filename, worksheet name, and rows.

```
  'excel|c:\readdata\[example6_5.xls]Group A!r2c1:r13c10';
data groupa;
```

Place the fileref for the worksheet in the INFILE statement.

```
  infile patients;
```

Read the rows with list input.

```
  input patient $ week_1 week_2 week_3 week_4 average;
run;
```

Specifying the DDE Triplet

The information inside single quotes in the FILENAME statement above is the DDE triplet. You write the triplet specifically for the application and file you want to read. There are three components to the triplet.

The *first component* is the application name. That value in this example is EXCEL. A vertical bar separates the first and second components.

The *second component* is called the topic, representing the topic of conversation between SAS and Microsoft Excel. The topic in this example here is the worksheet "Group A" in the EXAMPLE6_5 workbook. The filename of the workbook is enclosed in square brackets. An exclamation point separates the second and third components.

The *third component* is the range of conversation between SAS and Microsoft Excel, which is the range of cells that SAS should read. Here the third component tells SAS to start reading the worksheet at row 2 column one and read to row 13 column 10.

SAS starts reading on the second row and skips the first row, which contains the column names. The outermost cell with data is r13c6. Even though the upper range specified on the triplet is beyond r13c6, SAS does not add these empty cells to the data set.

Limitations of Using the DDE Access Method with Microsoft Excel

You must thoroughly understand the data that you want to read with DDE. There are limitations regarding the kinds of data values that you can read with DDE. SAS, by default, converts the tabs between the cells of a worksheet into blanks.

Problems can arise if the columns with character data also contain blanks. SAS then interprets a blank separating data within a cell as a delimiter between data values. The results of reading your worksheet would then be incorrect. To handle this situation, add the DELIMITER= and NOTAB options to your INFILE statement. The INFILE statement from the above example with these options would now look as follows.

```
infile patients delimiter='09'x notab;
```

The DELIMITER= option is set to the hexadecimal representation of the tab character. The NOTAB option tells SAS not to convert tabs sent from Excel to blanks. Under Windows, the value of the tab character is hexadecimal 09.

You must also take into consideration missing values. Missing values in your worksheet are blanks. If any of your cells are missing, add the DSD option to the INFILE statement as well as the DELIMITER=

and NOTAB options. The INFILE statement would now look as follows.

```
infile patients delimiter='09'x notab dsd;
```

The DSD option tells SAS to treat two consecutive delimiters, in this case two consecutive tab characters, as a missing value.

Accessing Applications Other than Microsoft Excel with DDE

You can also access applications other than Microsoft Excel with the DDE access method. This requires construction of the DDE triplet specifically for your application.

OLE may be a better method for communication between applications than DDE. In particular, passing commands between SAS and Microsoft Word 97 and later requires using Visual Basic for Applications statements. These applications are usually set up as part of a SAS/AF application using SAS Component Language (SCL).

Availability of the DDE Access Method

The DDE access method is part of Base SAS under Windows. You do not have to license additional products such as SAS/CONNECT to use the DDE access method.

Where to Go From Here

A more thorough discussion of using DDE with SAS is in the *SAS Companion for Microsoft Windows*. Topics covered include writing to another application and using hot links.

For information on OLE, refer to *SAS Component Language: Reference.*

For information on accessing worksheets with SAS/ACCESS, refer to *SAS/ACCESS for Relational Databases: Reference* (ODBC Chapter).

Example 6.6   Reading Data from a Web Page

Goal

From a local SAS session, access a web page and read data from the web page. The contents of the web page are in the form of an external file, which can be read into a data set.

Strategy

Specify in the FILENAME statement the web page address (the URL). Follow the fileref with the URL keyword to indicate that you will access the file with the URL access method.

Write a DATA step to read the external file. In the INFILE statements, reference the fileref assigned to the web page.

External File

This web page contains a report of orders and sales in 2002.

```
Orders Placed through Web Site in 2002
(number of orders, total sales)

    Jan 2002    402    $83,928
    Feb 2002    478    $193,283
    Mar 2002    350    $76,720
    Apr 2002    325    $65,391
    May 2002    366    $89,123
    Jun 2002    390    $81,538
    Jul 2002    303    $43,193
    Aug 2002    277    $38,651
    Sep 2002    463    $198,712
    Oct 2002    573    $236,423
    Nov 2002    629    $263,888
    Dec 2002    435    $173,028
```

The data values start on the fourth line of the report. The fields in the external file are column aligned and are in the following order:

1. month of sales

2. year of sales

3. number of orders

4. total sales in the month.

Resulting Data Set

Output 6.6 WEBSALES Data Set

```
            Web Site Sales in 2002 Read from Web Page

   Obs      monsales      yearsales      norders      salesamt

    1         Jan           2002           402        $83,928
    2         Feb           2002           478       $193,283
    3         Mar           2002           350        $76,720
    4         Apr           2002           325        $65,391
    5         May           2002           366        $89,123
    6         Jun           2002           390        $81,538
    7         Jul           2002           303        $43,193
    8         Aug           2002           277        $38,651
    9         Sep           2002           463       $198,712
   10         Oct           2002           573       $236,423
   11         Nov           2002           629       $263,888
   12         Dec           2002           435       $173,028
```

Program

This program accesses a web page and reads the data from the web page using the URL access method.

Assign a fileref to the URL of the web page. Follow the fileref with the access method.

```
filename webpage url
```

Specify the URL.

```
'http://intranet.abcco.com/websales/sales2002.dat';
data websales;
   infile webpage
```

Reference the fileref that points to the web page.

Skip the header lines and start reading the web page on the fourth data line.

```
         firstobs=4;
```

Read the web page data lines with list input and modified list input.

```
   input monsales $ yearsales norders
         salesamt : comma8.;
run;
proc print data=websales;
   title 'Web Site Sales in 2002 Read from Webpage';
   format salesamt dollar8.;
run;
```

A Closer Look

Specifying Options in the FILENAME Statement When Using the URL Access Method

There are additional options available with the URL access method. For example, if you know specific characteristics of the file you want to read, you may want to add these options to the FILENAME statement: BLOCKSIZE, LRECL and RECFM. If access to the web page requires a username and password, you can add the USER= and PASS= options to the FILENAME statement. Instead of PASS=, you can specify PROMPT so that when you execute the DATA step that reads the web page, you are then prompted to enter the password.

Availability of the URL Access Method

The URL access method is part of Base SAS. You do not have to license additional products such as SAS/CONNECT to use the URL access method.

Where to Go From Here

Refer to *SAS Language Reference: Dictionary*, for more complete information on reading a web page with the URL access method.

Example 6.7   Reading an XML Document

Goal

Create a data set from information stored in an XML document. The XML document was created with a different XML-based software package. It is well-formed and rectangular in structure. Note that the process of reading XML data into SAS may be part of a larger, web-based system. Therefore, XML files may be stored on a company webserver and may require special security privileges to access.

Strategy

Review the XML document to verify that it follows the physical structure that SAS requires.

Determine whether special security privileges are required to access the XML document.

Specify a LIBNAME statement that includes the XML engine keyword and the name of the XML document.

Write a DATA step that reads the XML document. Specify a SET statement that identifies the second-level instance tag that you want SAS to read. Write the reference to the tag as though it is a SAS data set. Use the libname defined on the LIBNAME statement as the library name. Use the second-level instance tag name as the data set name.

In this example, read two second-level instance tags from the XML document and concatenate them into one data set.

Existing XML Document

This document contains information about stocks that two clients hold.

```
<?xml version="1.0" ?>

<TABLE>
    <Client1>
        <COMPANY> ABC Inc. </COMPANY>
        <PRICE1998> 38.90 </PRICE1998>
        <PRICE1999> 43.50 </PRICE1999>
        <PRICE2000> 22.20 </PRICE2000>
    </CLIENT1>
    <CLIENT1>
        <COMPANY> Mighty Movers </COMPANY>
        <PRICE1998> 16.20 </PRICE1998>
        <PRICE1999> 22.50 </PRICE1999>
        <PRICE2000> 26.80 </PRICE2000>
        <PRICE2001> 20.10 </PRICE2001>
        <PRICE2002> 21.20 </PRICE2002>
        <PRICE2003> 24.60 </PRICE2003>
    </CLIENT1>
```

```
<CLIENT1>
   <COMPANY> Wireless Wonders </COMPANY>
   <PRICE2001> 5.70 </PRICE2001>
   <PRICE2002> 25.00 </PRICE2002>
   <PRICE2003> 45.60 </PRICE2003>
</CLIENT1>
<CLIENT1>
   <COMPANY> Metro Office Supplies </COMPANY>
   <PRICE1998> 63.30 </PRICE1998>
   <PRICE1999> 68.40 </PRICE1999>
   <PRICE2000> 74.10 </PRICE2000>
   <PRICE2001> 55.00 </PRICE2001>
   <PRICE2002> 41.70 </PRICE2002>
</CLIENT1>
<Client2>
   <COMPANY> Great Lakes Vegetables </COMPANY>
   <PRICE1999> 21.70 </PRICE1999>
   <PRICE2000> 17.80 </PRICE2000>
   <PRICE2001> 16.00 </PRICE2001>
   <PRICE2002> 25.40 </PRICE2002>
   <PRICE2003> 22.20 </PRICE2003>
</CLIENT2>
<CLIENT 2>
   <COMPANY> All Health Inc. </COMPANY>
   <PRICE2003> 16.20 </PRICE 2003>
</CLIENT 2>
</TABLE>
```

The root-enclosing element of an XML document is the document container. SAS translates this to a library. The root-enclosing element in this document is TABLE.

The second-level instance tags, CLIENT1 and CLIENT2, each become a SAS data set name.

Each instance of the second-level tag becomes an observation. The elements within each second-level tag become the variables of the data set. SAS creates seven variables from this XML document: COMPANY, PRICE1998, PRICE1999, PRICE2000, PRICE2001, PRICE2002, and PRICE2003.

Resulting Data Set

Output 6.7 PROC PRINT of
TWOCLIENTS Data Set

```
                    Stocks Held by Two Clients 1998-2003

        Obs    PRICE2003     PRICE2002      PRICE2001   PRICE2000    PRICE1999

         1         .             .              .          22.20       43.50
         2       24.60         21.20          20.10        26.80       22.50
         3       45.60         25.00           5.70          .           .
         4         .           41.70          55.00        74.10       68.40
         5       22.20         25.40          16.00        17.80       21.70
         6       16.20           .              .            .           .


        Obs    PRICE1998     COMPANY                      client      yrsheld

         1       38.90       ABC Inc.                       1            3
         2       16.20       Mighty Movers                  1            6
         3         .         Wireless Wonders               1            3
         4       63.30       Metro Office Supplies          1            5
         5         .         Great Lakes Vegetables         2            5
         6         .         All Health Inc.                2            1
```

Programs

This DATA step creates a SAS data set from a well-formed XML document. Each of the two second-level instance tags in the document becomes a data set. The two data sets are concatenated in the DATA step.

Specify the engine that the LIBNAME statement should use.

```
libname mystocks xml
```

Identify the XML document that you want SAS to read.

```
            'c:\readdata\stockprices.xml';
```

Read each of the second-level instance tags in the XML document as a SAS data set and concatenate them. Define two variables that can be tested to determine whether the data set contributed to the current observation.

```
data twoclients;
   set mystocks.client1(in=in1)
       mystocks.client2(in=in2);
```

Define a new variable based on the values of the IN= variables.

```
    if in1 then client=1;
    else if in2 then client=2;

    yrsheld=n(of price1998-price2003);
run;
proc print data=twoclients;
    title "Stocks Held by Two Clients 1998-2003";
run;
```

Where to Go From Here

The example above is a simple application of creating data sets from an XML document. Information on how to access XML documents with SAS is published on the SAS web site at http://www.sas.com. For example, on the website you can find additional information on the XML document structure that SAS requires as well as information on the options available to read more complex XML documents.

Index

Call your local SAS office to order these books
from Books by Users Press

www.sas.com/pubs

*Welcome * Bienvenue * Willkommen * Yohkoso * Bienvenido*

SAS Publishing Is Easy to Reach

Visit our Web site located at www.sas.com/pubs

You will find product and service details, including

- **companion Web sites**
- **sample chapters**
- **tables of contents**
- **author biographies**
- **book reviews**

Learn about

- **regional user-group conferences**
- **trade-show sites and dates**
- **authoring opportunities**
- **e-books**

Explore all the services that SAS Publishing has to offer!

Your Listserv Subscription Automatically Brings the News to You

Do you want to be among the first to learn about the latest books and services available from SAS Publishing? Subscribe to our listserv **newdocnews-l** and, once each month, you will automatically receive a description of the newest books and which environments or operating systems and SAS® release(s) each book addresses.

To subscribe,

1. Send an e-mail message to **listserv@vm.sas.com**.

2. Leave the "Subject" line blank.

3. Use the following text for your message:

   subscribe NEWDOCNEWS-L *your-first-name your-last-name*

   For example: subscribe NEWDOCNEWS-L John Doe

You're Invited to Publish with SAS Institute's Books by Users Press

If you enjoy writing about SAS software and how to use it, the Books by Users program at SAS Institute offers a variety of publishing options. We are actively recruiting authors to publish books and sample code.

If you find the idea of writing a book by yourself a little intimidating, consider writing with a co-author. Keep in mind that you will receive complete editorial and publishing support, access to our users, technical advice and assistance, and competitive royalties. Please ask us for an author packet at **sasbbu@sas.com** or call 919-531-7447. See the Books by Users Web page at **www.sas.com/bbu** for complete information.

Book Discount Offered at SAS Public Training Courses!

When you attend one of our SAS Public Training Courses at any of our regional Training Centers in the United States, you will receive a 20% discount on book orders that you place during the course. Take advantage of this offer at the next course you attend!

SAS Institute Inc.
SAS Campus Drive
Cary, NC 27513-2414
Fax 919-677-4444

E-mail: sasbook@sas.com
Web page: www.sas.com/pubs
To order books, call SAS Publishing Sales at 800-727-3228*
For other SAS business, call 919-677-8000*

* Note: Customers outside the United States should contact their local SAS office.

The Power to Know.

§sas | SAS Publishing